GLADIATOR

GLADIATOR
THE MAKING OF THE RIDLEY SCOTT EPIC

INTRODUCTION BY **RIDLEY SCOTT**
FOREWORD BY **WALTER PARKES**

EDITED BY **DIANA LANDAU**   DESIGNED BY **TIMOTHY SHANER**
CONTRIBUTING WRITER **SHARON BLACK**

DREAMWORKS

A NEWMARKET PICTORIAL MOVIEBOOK

B⊞XTREE

First published 2000 by Newmarket Press, New York, New York 10017

This edition published 2000 by Boxtree
an imprint of Macmillan Publishers Ltd
25 Eccleston Place London SW1W 9NF
Basingstoke and Oxford

www.macmillan.com

Associated companies throughout the world

ISBN 0 7522 7264 0

Unless otherwise credited, all production photographs by Jaap Buitendijk.
Motion picture artwork and photos TM & © 2000 DreamWorks LLC and Universal Studios.
Cover Key Art, Creative Director: David Sameth. Cover Key Art, Art Director: Jeff Bacon.
DreamWorks Art Director: Paul Elliott.

Page 1: Tigris of Gaul mask, drawn by Sylvain Despretz.
Pages 12 and 116: Part-opening artwork by production illustrator Denis Rich.

Acknowledgment of permission to reprint previously
copyrighted material is found on page 160.

Portions of the text of this book are adapted from the *Gladiator* production
notes by Sharon Black, and from original articles by Joe Fordham that
appeared in *VFXPro*, an online publication of Creative Planet Inc.
For the complete articles, go to vfxpro.com

1 3 5 7 9 8 6 4 2

A CIP catalogue record for this book is available from the British Library.

CONTENTS

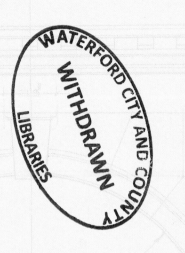

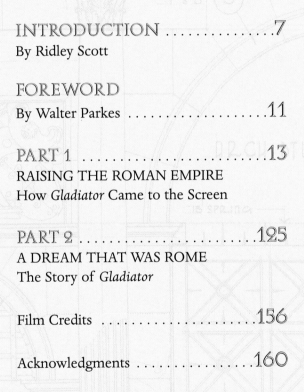

BY RIDLEY SCOTT

When Walter Parkes and Doug Wick showed me a reproduction of the Jean-Léon Gérôme painting *Pollice Verso* ("Thumbs Down"), it was the perfect rendition of a glimpse of Roman life—the proportions, the architecture, the light and shadow, everything. "Didn't toga-and-sandal films die out 40 years ago?" What a fascinating world to revisit—I was hooked.

We are in an era where we're re-examining everything that's come before, and revisiting classic subjects. The Roman Empire has interested storytellers from Shakespeare to Stanley Kubrick. The Romans brought us literature, engineering, art and architecture, law and government. They built everywhere they went. Their armies were both stonemasons and warriors; all over Europe and throughout the Mediterranean their physical presence is still there to see. How could a civilization that achieved so much in cultural terms also

"I love to create worlds, and every facet of that world has to work within the rules of the story. You must smell the battleground and experience the beauty and light of the golden city. The film must take you into this world, so that you become part of 175 A.D."

— RIDLEY SCOTT

have this barbaric legacy of gladiatorial games?

We needed to revisit this world without it being a history lesson and to interpret these historical figures in a way that made sense to audiences today. Filmmaking 40 years ago tended to treat these subjects with a theatricality that wouldn't be appropriate now.

Story and character are the two most important elements in any movie, and I wanted to get close to the characters and see real people with real issues.

Finding a great cast is critical to give weight and substance to a story, and Russell Crowe made us really believe in Maximus and a hero's journey.

LEFT: Ridley Scott beneath the entrance to Proximo's gladiator compound in the Rome set (Malta). ABOVE: A *Gladiator* camera crew works on a crane shot of Praetorian Guards marching through the Roman forum.

Just as effective in their roles were Joaquin Phoenix as the emotionally wounded Commodus, Connie Nielsen as Lucilla, the late Oliver Reed playing Proximo, Richard Harris as Marcus Aurelius, and Derek Jacobi as Gracchus.

I love to create worlds, and every facet of that world has to work within the rules of the story. You must smell the battleground and experience the beauty and light of the golden city. The film must take you into this world, so that you become part of 175 A.D.

Inevitably, there are comparisons in sport and movie entertainment to the Romans and their spectacles in the arena. Mass entertainment provides a visceral experience of things you can't have, or can't do. "Escapism" is a word with bad connotations. I prefer "transported," "elevated,"

or "taken on a journey"! The film's perspective on the games had many levels—showing their popularity, their savagery, but also giving insight into the political motives for the games.

On the production side, I was fortunate to have some of the best people in the industry helping me recreate the Roman Empire as I envisioned it. My colleagues in production design, cinematography, editing, music scoring, costumes, stunts, and effects excelled themselves. Like General Maximus, I couldn't have taken the journey without them. When we were almost through with post-production, I remember saying to Walter and Doug that I feel as if we had built Rome and fought all the battles from the Danube to North Africa and back to Rome.

Like Rome, it certainly wasn't made in a day.

FOREWORD

BY WALTER PARKES

Sometimes the biggest movies come together in small but key moments.

We waited in the cavernous modern office filled with Moroccan antiques. After working on the script for nearly a year, producer Doug Wick and I had come to ask Ridley Scott to direct *Gladiator*. We brought with us David Franzoni's second-draft screenplay along with a color reproduction of a French painting from the nineteenth century. After a few minutes, Doug and I were shown into Ridley's office, where I launched into a discussion of the further revisions we intended for the script. But as I spoke, I noticed that Ridley's eyes kept wandering back to the image.

The painting, *Pollice Verso* by Jean-Léon Gérôme, depicts the defining moment of a battle in the Colosseum. A gladiator, his face obscured by an impossibly large helmet, stands over his opponent and looks to the Emperor for the final verdict. But while the subject is familiar, the treatment is not. Gérôme depicts ancient Rome in the colors and stylizations of his own imagination and his own time. Gone is the harsh Mediterranean light; instead, deep shadows play across the scene. The massive stone edges of the Colosseum have been softened by Turkish fabrics and Persian rugs. And, according to Gérôme, the women of Rome favored diaphanous gowns in rich hues rather than the pristine white or saffron robes we see painted on the pottery that survives from that time.

Simply put, the painting is history as interpreted by a singular artist of his time—as is the film *Gladiator*. The Rome that Ridley Scott created was painstakingly researched, to be sure—but it was also imagined. From the fascist-overtoned armor of the Praetorian Guard to the flowing manes of every horse (an early direction specified no clipped manes) to the rose petals that cover the arena floor for the final confrontation, Ridley's signature can be seen on every frame. Yet somehow, the visual style never became an end in itself; all the attention to detail ultimately served the more important values of story, theme, and character. And for all of its size—locations on three continents, hundreds of crew members, at times thousands of extras—*Gladiator* is an intimate story, told on a human scale. It's the work of a true artist at the peak of his powers.

When I had finished my pitch, Ridley simply pointed to the picture and said, "I can do that."

And he did.

ABOVE: Laurie MacDonald and Walter Parkes, executive producers of *Gladiator*.

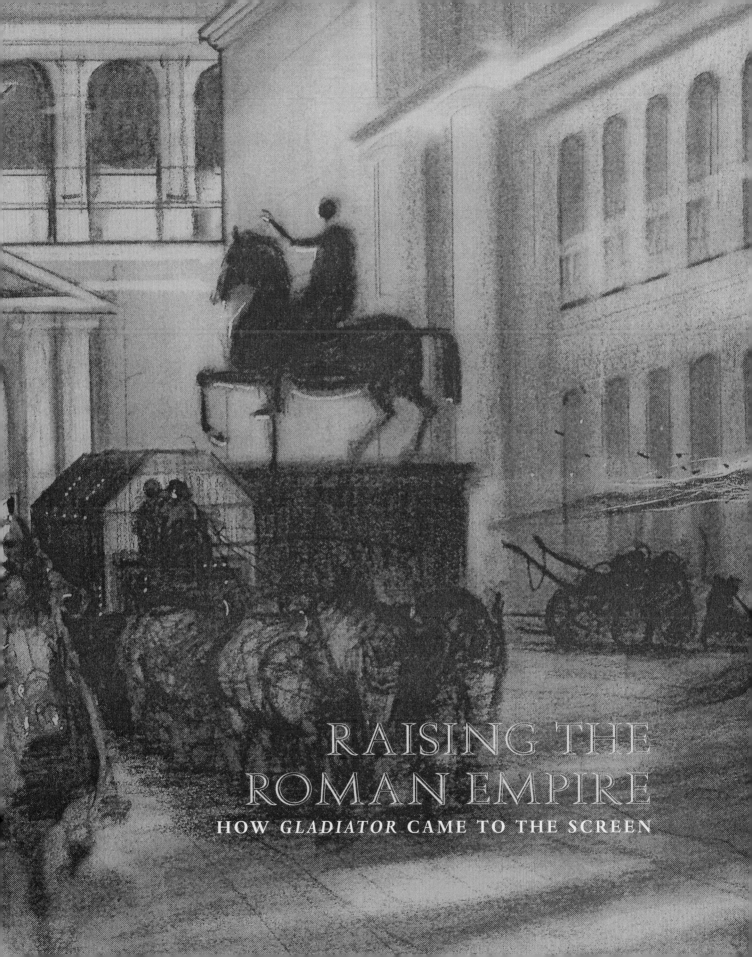

RAISING THE ROMAN EMPIRE
HOW *GLADIATOR* CAME TO THE SCREEN

"LET THE GAMES BEGIN"

In 1996, the film industry had its imaginative sights set on the future. Dramatic advances in digital special effects technology in the last decade had enhanced filmmakers' ability to create "event movies" that realized science-fiction visions and supernatural fantasies in incredible scope and detail. Scores of movies about space exploration, or aliens assaulting Earth, or disaster hurtling towards us from space were opening or in production. Visions of summer-blockbuster nirvana orbited around interplanetary combat and cool futuristic hardware, as they had since *Star Wars*.

While other cinematic creators were envisioning what lies ahead, screenwriter David Franzoni came to DreamWorks SKG with a story about gladiators in ancient Rome—a world that had more or less vanished from movie screens in the early 1960s under the weight of draped togas, smashed chariots, and Cleopatra eyeliner. Franzoni's story would be set not in the glittering reaches of far galaxies but in the stony arenas and palaces of a crumbling civilization. It would feature not 23rd-century heroes piloting starships and brandishing laser weapons, but long-dead and unremembered slaves fighting for their lives in the bloody dust with short sword and dagger.

Franzoni had already shown his flair for bringing the past vividly to life, having written the Steven Spielberg-directed saga *Amistad* for DreamWorks a few years earlier. Franzoni dramatized a later period in the HBO film *Citizen Cohn*, starring James Woods, for which he won the 1992 George Foster Peabody Award, the Cable ACE Award, and the 1993 Pen West Literary Award. So his idea about gladiators commanded serious attention from DreamWorks production executives Walter Parkes and Laurie MacDonald, and producer Douglas Wick of Red Wagon Films.

Wick says, "David's idea was to do a story set in the ancient Roman arena, which was really at the epicenter of their whole culture. Once we began to study the period, we realized that the arena was the perfect peephole into that world. It brought together all the strata of Roman society, from the emperor and the senators and aristocrats down to the lower classes and slaves. The best minds of the age were put to work in building arenas, designing all the peripheral machinery needed, in tending and transporting all the animals that were used. The arena was such a priority in the culture that it spawned all kinds of breakthroughs in engineering, drainage, metalwork, and so on.

"And we came to realize that it had a lot of modern relevance. It was all about theater, about distraction—a way to control the populace."

DreamWorks became an active partner in the project from the very start, with Parkes working with Wick and Franzoni to develop the story. As the richness of the ancient world and the drama of the arena unfolded during their research, they became ever more convinced in the power of the subject to "bring audiences around the globe into

"Once we began to study the period, we realized that the arena was the perfect peephole into that world . . . it was all about theater, about distraction—a way to control the populace."

— PRODUCER DOUGLAS WICK

an amazing other world," says Wick.

"No one had done this kind of spectacle in 30 years," Wick points out. "It was an opportunity that hadn't been visited in a long time. We felt that audiences were getting tired of space movies, and that to revisit Rome was to take them to extraordinary spectacle, extraordinary action—but all grounded in a human reality. And with the new technology, you could give them a much more realistic version than ever seen before."

TRANSCENDING THE TOGA

The film industry has had a longstanding love affair with the ancient world, and the Roman Empire in particular. From D. W. Griffith's *Intolerance* to Monty Python's *Life of Brian*, visions of the imperial pomp and pageantry have taken many forms. Henry Koster's *The Robe* and Cecil B. DeMille's *The Ten Commandments* took a Judeo-Christian slant on ancient history. *Fellini's Satyricon* focused on the sensual decadence of Rome during its decline. Several epic rousers of the 1950s and '60s—*Quo Vadis?*, *Ben Hur*, and *Spartacus*—relied on action, drama, and the best special effects available at the time.

Some of these efforts were critical and box-office hits, notably Stanley Kubrick's *Spartacus* (1950), the stirring tale of a Thracian slave (Kirk Douglas) who led a briefly successful revolt against Roman forces in 71 B.C. Staggering battle scenes, superb cinematography, and sparkling performances by British legends Laurence Olivier, Charles Laughton, and Peter Ustinov were among its highlights, and Ridley Scott acknowledges his debt to Kubrick in making *Gladiator*—especially the care he brought to fully realizing each moment of film. "Kubrick was always very specific, very carefully worked out," he says.

Other tales of the ancient world were less successful: the Liz Taylor / Richard Burton *Cleopatra* in 1965 didn't live up to pre-release expectations. In the 1962 *Barabbas*, directed by Richard Fleischer and starring Anthony Quinn, a good script and lavish production values were buried by the film's length. Also in the category of interesting failures was Anthony Mann's 1964 film *The Fall of the*

LEFT: Promotional still from *Quo Vadis?* with Robert Taylor and Deborah Kerr. ABOVE: Poster art for MGM's 1959 blockbuster *Ben-Hur.* OPPOSITE: Kirk Douglas as Spartacus confronts a foe in the arena; behind him is the emperor's box

19

Roman Empire, whose plot featured several of the main characters who later appeared in *Gladiator*.

Whatever the plot or level of filmmaking ambition, the indispensable ingredients generally were epic scale, mammoth sets, vast armies of extras, and acres of flowing robes, all too often exposing less-than-impressive actorly knees. And the actors tapped to portray athletes, heroes, chariot drivers, or biblical strongmen, while sometimes in decent physical shape, left a lot to the imagination. When Ridley Scott was first asked to consider *Gladiator*, one writer speculates, "Images of a loincloth-clad Victor Mature sucking in his gut must have flashed through [his] head." As the end of the 20th century neared, the appearance of full-out spoofs like *A Funny Thing Happened on the Way to the Forum* and *Life of Brian* made it clear that the genre had by now descended (or ascended) into the realm of camp. "Do you like gladiator movies" was even used as a punchline by Peter Graves in *Airplane*.

For the filmmakers contemplating David Franzoni's story, knowing all this could have induced an incurable case of "toga fear." But there was very little of that in planning for *Gladiator*, Douglas Wick insists—though it did

ABOVE: Duncan Regehr as a gladiator in the 1984 British mini-series of *The Last Days of Pompeii* (the tale was also filmed in 1935 and 1960). BELOW: Charlton Heston steers his way toward an Oscar® with his portrayal of the title character in *Ben-Hur*.

guide some of their thinking. "The more we looked into the story and the period, and the more fascinating and intelligent details we discovered, the less fearful we were of a toga version," he recalls.

Some of the filmmakers' goals emerged from thinking about what they *didn't* want for the movie. What they did want was a totally convincing level of detail in the settings, breathtaking realism in the action scenes, and powerful but contained acting from true actors—not necessarily "movie stars." They knew they would have a huge advantage over earlier films in the level of production values that could be achieved by a top-flight design team, and in the extent to which the realism of settings and action could be enhanced with the magic of digital effects.

Beyond that, says Wick, "our primary challenge was getting the story right. And even more than that, it was director, director, director— because in the hands of a mediocre director, there's always a little bit of the toga fear."

REEL LIFE IN THE ANCIENT WORLD

Barabbas (1962) Based on the Pär Lagerkvist novel, with Anthony Quinn and Jack Palance, this saga of the criminal released by Pontius Pilate in place of Jesus is wordy but worthy.

Ben-Hur (1959) Archetypal Hollywood epic of the Jewish hero Ben-Hur (Charlton Heston) won a record 11 Oscars. Directed by William Wyler; special effects and matte vistas by A. Arnold Gillespie and Peter Ellenshaw. A 1926 version starring Ramon Novarro and Francis X. Bushman was the biggest silent-film spectacle ever.

Cleopatra (1963) Interminable (4-hour) retelling of the Cleopatra/Julius Caesar/Marc Antony triangle, best remembered for sparking the off-screen affair of Elizabeth Taylor and Richard Burton. Joseph L. Mankiewicz directed.

The Fall of the Roman Empire (1964) Alec Guinness is Marcus Aurelius, Sophia Loren is Lucilla, and Christopher Plummer is Commodus, but Anthony Mann's intelligent film was lost on most sixties audiences.

A Funny Thing Happened on the Way to the Forum (1966) Richard Lester adapted the madcap Broadway musical; stars Zero Mostel as a conniving slave. Score by Stephen Sondheim.

Intolerance (1916) D. W. Griffith's landmark epic weaves four stories of prejudice and inhumanity, the first set in ancient Babylon with spectacular sets and crowd scenes.

Life of Brian (1979) The Pythons' giddy tale of Brian, whose life parallels Christ's, is an equal-opportunity offender; highlights include Pontius Pilate with a gay lisp.

Quo Vadis? (1951) Romance between Roman soldier (Robert Taylor) and Christian (Deborah Kerr) during reign of Nero; some gladiatorial scenes and fine location shooting.

The Robe (1953) Richard Burton is the Roman centurion who oversees Christ's crucifixion and has his life changed. First film shot in CinemaScope. Its 1954 sequel, *Demetrius and the Gladiators*, starred Victor Mature.

Fellini's Satyricon (1970) Visually enthralling, sometimes perverse, Fellini's take on Roman decadence parades an array of bizarre characters.

Spartacus (1960) Kubrick's full-out spectacle won Oscars for art direction, costume design, cinematography, and screenplay (by Dalton Trumbo), as well as Best Supporting Actor for Peter Ustinov. VFX designer Saul Bass and stunt coordinator Yakima Canutt collaborated on the battle scenes.

The Ten Commandments (1923, 1956) Cecil B. DeMille filmed the biblical epic twice: in 1923 and the 1956 version with Charlton Heston as Moses, Yul Brynner as Pharaoh, and a huge cast. Parting of the Red Sea was among the outstanding special effects created in bluescreen by Farçiot Edouart.

RIDLEY SCOTT: CREATING WORLDS

Once screenwriter Franzoni and producers Wick and Parkes began to focus on their story, their excitement escalated about the film's potential—in the hands of the right director. The kind of person they had in mind would have to be a "master visualist." And, says Wick, "the fantasy person was always Ridley Scott."

Knowing that the man they were after was the quintessential cinematic visualist—the director responsible for such indelible film visions as *Alien*, *Blade Runner*, and *Thelma & Louise*—they used a powerful image as bait. Before even asking Scott to read the screenplay in progress, they put before him a copy of Jean-Léon Gérôme's 1872 painting *Pollice Verso* ("Thumbs Down"). This dramatic scene (see page 24) puts the viewer at ground level in the Roman Colosseum at the instant when a fearsomely costumed gladiator, foot on his fallen opponent's throat, looks up to the throngs surrounding the emperor's box giving the fatal gesture that dooms his enemy to

BELOW: Pre-production sketch by Ridley Scott of the approach to the Colosseum. OPPOSITE: The director on the Germania set, Bourne Woods in Farnham, England. OVERLEAF: *Pollice Verso* ("Thumbs Down") by Jean-Léon Gérôme, 1872. Courtesy the Phoenix Art Museum. The French painter and sculptor Gérôme was an orientalist who packed his pictures with authentic detail gleaned from several visits to Egypt and Istanbul.

death. You can practically feel the hot sand in the sun-and-shadow-streaked arena, smell the blood that soaks it, and hear the crowd's bloodthirsty roar, so vivid is the artist's rendering.

"That image spoke to me of the Roman Empire in all its glory and wickedness," says Scott. "Because what I love to do—apart from getting a good script and making movies—where I enjoy myself most, I think, is creating worlds. Sometimes new worlds, i.e., science fiction, or recreating a world that's historical."

Moviegoers probably think first of Ridley Scott in connection with science fiction, thanks to the phenomenal success of *Alien* (1979), which catapulted Sigourney Weaver to stardom, and the groundbreaking *Blade Runner* (1982, with a critically acclaimed director's cut released in 1993). As influential in its own realm was the futuristic vision Scott created for a landmark Apple Macintosh TV commercial in 1984—inspired by George Orwell's *1984*.

But Scott's forays into recreating history have been equally distinguished, if not as well known. He won a Golden Globe in 2000 for his work as a producer on the HBO movie *RKO 281*,

LEFT: Ridley Scott's sketch of the gates of Rome. ABOVE: The Felix Legions advance on the enemy in Germania. OPPOSITE ABOVE: City gate, drawing by Ridley Scott.

"It's great for an actor to work with a guy like Ridley Scott, who is so in command of his profession and his craft, and who knows precisely what he wants. That is a gift for an actor because half your problems are gone. And if you have someone off camera like Ridley, you have to trust him."

— RICHARD HARRIS

which dramatized the making of Orson Welles's *Citizen Kane*. He debuted as director in feature films with the period drama *The Duellists*, which won the Best First Film Award at Cannes and which has entered the classics repertory. And in 1992 he directed and produced *1492: Conquest of Paradise*, starring Gerard Depardieu as Christopher Columbus in an ambitious retelling of the explorer's discovery of the Americas.

Scott's mastery of the visual language of film is no accident; he is a graduate of London's prestigious Royal College of Art. He began his directing career at the BBC doing commercials before moving into features. Recent directing credits include *GI Jane*, starring Demi Moore as the first woman Navy SEAL; *White Squall*, starring Jeff Bridges; the gritty crime drama *Black Rain*, with Michael Douglas and Andy Garcia; the romantic thriller *Someone to Watch Over Me*; and the fantasy *Legend*, which starred Tom Cruise. He has also produced several of the films he directed, as well as *The Browning Version*, *Clay Pigeons*, and *Where the Money Is*, starring Paul Newman. He is currently directing *Hannibal*, the sequel to the Oscar-winning Best Picture *Silence of the Lambs*, starring Anthony Hopkins in the title role.

Scott welcomed the chance to explore another historical world. "God knows we have had an abundance of science fiction lately; everybody's been there, seen it and done it. So to do a science fiction movie today is getting more difficult—how are you going to present the world so it

ABOVE: The crew films a tracking shot of chariots in the Carthage Battle scene in the partial Colosseum set. OPPOSITE: Ridley Scott and Russell Crowe confer in the Morocco arena set.

looks different and fresh? With history, your challenge, really, is to see how accurate you can be. It's to do with research and choosing the right people: the right production designer, the right costume designer, the right armorer, and so on. And of course you have to do massive research.

"Every film has its own difficulties built into it—the thing is not to let them get through the door and start to control you. Again, it's to do with creating a team, the choice of the people who are doing things for you; with delegation and making decisions. This wasn't difficult; it was enjoyable. I mean, how often do you get to build

> "The idea of taking the Ridley Scott tour through the world of ancient Rome just made us want to get right on that bus."
>
> —DOUGLAS WICK

the Colosseum and a North African Roman town and the Forum, or stage the German front on the Danube with thousands of Roman troops fighting the German barbarians? Not very often, today, particularly. And I really enjoyed the magnitude of it."

Despite his enthusiasm for the project, Scott was aware that he was venturing into a genre whose popularity had not been tested in this generation. "*Spartacus* was 40 years ago," the director observes, "and *Ben-Hur* was even before that. These movies were part of my cinema-going youth. But at the dawn of the new millennium, I thought this might be the ideal time to revisit what may have been the most important period of the last two thousand years—if not all recorded history—the apex and beginning of the decline of the greatest military and political power the world has ever known."

CRAFTING THE TALE

"Our story suggests that, should a hero arise out of the carnage of the arena, his popularity would give him tremendous power."

—RIDLEY SCOTT

Once the production's ideal director was on board, the team went back to work on the all-important story. Story and script development for *Gladiator* was a fluid and dynamic process that went on for several years, right up until the last frames were edited. This was in part because of Ridley Scott's highly visual approach to moviemaking. Nothing in the script is set in stone, and what finally ends up on the screen is wholly dependent on what he sees—first in the storyboarding process and later through his camera. The final screen image is a product of many factors that evolve along the way: locations, production design, casting choices, weather conditions, and a thousand other variables. "There are nuances in the script that develop as Ridley sees the character developing," observed the late Oliver Reed, who plays the gladiator trainer Proximo.

Several accomplished writers had a hand in scripting *Gladiator*. David Franzoni developed the story in conjunction with Douglas Wick, executive producers Walter Parkes and Laurie MacDonald, and the director, and drafted the original screenplay; and as one of the producers he remained involved all the way through to the final cut. " My vision from the beginning was this is not *Ben-Hur*. It's *All Quiet on the Western Front*," says Franzoni. "This is a grownup movie about war, death, and life in Rome—the life of a gladiator."

Collaborating on the screenplay at different times were screenwriters John Logan and William Nicholson. Logan, who co-wrote the screenplay (from his own story) for Oliver Stone's football drama *Any Given Sunday*, also wrote the HBO movie *RKO 281*, produced by Ridley Scott. Currently he is working on a script about the life of Howard Hughes for director Michael Mann, and the screenplay for a remake of H. G. Wells's *The Time Machine*, a DreamWorks/Warner Bros. co-production. William Nicholson was nominated for an Academy Award for his screenplay for *Shadowlands*, based on his original stage play and starring Anthony Hopkins and Debra Winger. His other film writing credits include *Nell*, starring Jodie Foster; *First Knight*, with Sean Connery, Richard Gere, and Julia Ormond; and *Sarafina!* starring Whoopie Goldberg.

But even though countless details of the story were tweaked along the way, a few essential ideas remained at the film's heart. Starting with the dramatic core of gladiatorial combat, the creators had to decide which period during Rome's centuries-long dominion to focus on. For this and other period research tasks they turned to Suzanne Jurva, then head of DreamWorks research department and to experts in Roman civilization.

The search led to a time near the end of the second century A.D., around the death of the revered emperor Marcus Aurelius and the accession of his son Commodus—a moment scholars

ABOVE: Ridley Scott and Russell Crowe (as Maximus) in the North African slave market. RIGHT: Producer Douglas Wick.

ABOVE: Ridley Scott and Oliver Reed, who played the gladiator trainer Proximo. OPPOSITE: *Gladiator* audiences came to recognize Maximus's signature gesture: rubbing earth between his hands before a major fight.

"The writers did a lot of experimenting. There are nuances in the script that develop as Ridley sees the character developing."

—OLIVER REED

generally identify as a turning point, when Rome had passed its apex of achievement and was beginning to decline. It was also a time when, for about a century, gladiatorial games enjoyed their greatest popularity. (Just one of the many contrasts between Marcus Aurelius and Commodus was that the former had little use for the games, while Commodus not only loved blood sports but was among the few emperors actually to engage in combat in the arena.)

This time was "the beginning of the end of the Roman Empire," notes Ridley Scott, "which was reflected in what went on in the arenas. There you saw the sickness of Rome, how Rome had become corpulent, how Rome had stopped looking at the far reaches of the Empire." He notes that, "Entertainment has frequently been used by leaders as a means to distract an abused citizenry. The most tyrannical ruler must still beguile his people even as he brutalizes them. The gladiatorial games were such a distraction. Our story suggests that, should a hero arise out of the carnage of the arena, his popularity would give him tremendous power . . . and were he to be a genuine champion of the people, he might threaten even the most absolute tyrant."

And that brings us to the heart of the matter, the human drama every story needs. Douglas Wick says the filmmakers "tried to find a hero's journey that would maximize the experience of the arena for audiences. The soul of the movie was always Maximus—a Roman general who at the height of his triumph is thrown from power, ending up as a slave and then forced to fight in the arena, a kind of parody of what he did as a great warrior."

From this idea for a protagonist, the writers fleshed out a man who is commanding yet down to earth, a warrior who would rather be a family man and farmer, a Spaniard and foreigner who nonetheless embodies a fierce loyalty to Rome and what it stands for. This character would ultimately spring to life in Russell Crowe's white-hot performance.

"Where the journey got really exciting," says Douglas Wick, "was when Ridley Scott became the tour guide. It became clear that he was going to take the audience into the reality of what it would have been like to be a gladiator. We'd bring up any aspect of the journey, and he'd start to conjure up details, literally sketch them. He was always after the kind of specificity that keeps it interesting: what conditions would have been like, where they slept, what they ate. What it's like to fight in a provincial, small-town arena and then see the likes of Rome and the Colosseum."

Not unlike his hero Maximus, director Scott bore a general's responsibility for the full scope of the endeavor, from the big picture down to the minutest details—a task that his prior experience with epic-scale movies had prepared him for well. So even while the bones of script, character, and event were being forged, he was mapping out in pre-production what it would take to translate them to the screen in most spectacular fashion: the settings, the sets, the extras, the battle choreography, the costumes, the swordplay, and finally the computer graphics that would knit all the action together.

As a visual artist, one of his primary tools for envisioning and experimenting with scenes and shots was storyboard drawings. For many months before principal photography began, Scott worked on his own making rough sketches of key scenes. Then he collaborated for several months more with storyboard artist Sylvain Despretz, expanding, revising, refining, discarding ideas, trying out new ones. (See the accompanying sidebar.) For *Gladiator*, it was the first major step from concepts on paper to what would be seen on the screen.

ABOVE: Preliminary sketches by Ridley Scott of the scene called Maximus's Journey. BELOW: A different version of the same scene drawn by Sylvain Despretz.

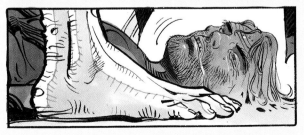

THE DIRECTOR AND THE STORYBOARD ARTIST

Storyboard artist Sylvain Despretz collaborated closely with Ridley Scott on *Gladiator*. Here's how he describes the process:

"Ridley gets involved with pre-production months and months before most directors will. Several months out he will give very detailed sketches—shot by shot, blow by blow. His sketches are as much about light, depth and composition as they are about action. A couple of weeks out, the sketches get very rough and the instructions very loose, because he just doesn't have time. By then you've usually got the gist of where the film is going and can improvise quite a bit. But generally Ridley is extraordinarily specific. He knows pretty much everything he wants to put in his film. Having said that, he's very open to ideas—particularly in action scenes where several people sit around and ask, 'what if this happens?' But for me the most interesting part is having him direct the storyboard, because at the time we do it, of course, these are the only images of the film anyone will see for quite a while. There's this brief moment when you're being directed by the director and you're making the first version of his film. It's quite a rush.

"Ridley changes his mind a lot and sometimes uses the storyboard to get rid of ideas rather than lock them in. The fact that he has storyboarded heavily only means that he got a first shot out of his system, so to speak—as when an artist does studies. Ridley gives himself the luxury to explore the picture with his art department. In fact, he's quite loose. He shoots with five, six, seven cameras sometimes, and can be quite spontaneous. I can't say the storyboard particularly resembles the final film.

"The storyboard can only be as good as its director. I think a director like Ridley is an artist, a draftsman, somebody who can really sketch in terms of composition, shape, depth of field, everything. It's great fun to work with a director who can really express himself visually."

TOP: Storyboards for the Carthage Battle are posted in the Colosseum set as the crew sets up a shot. ABOVE: Artist Sylvain Despretz holds the Tiger mask, based on his drawing. OVERLEAF: The death of Commodus, production drawing by Sylvain Despretz.

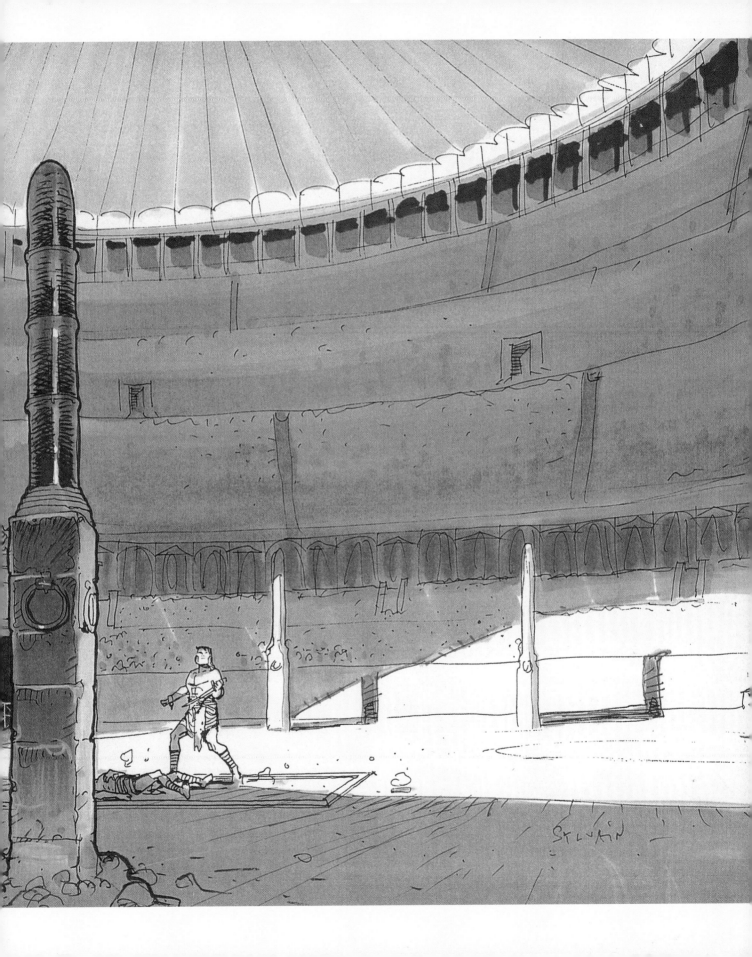

ROME IN THE SECOND CENTURY

At the time *Gladiator* takes place, the Roman Empire was nearing the end of a long period of stability and success known as the Pax Romana. The emperors who had reigned since the end of the first century—Trajan, Hadrian, Antoninus Pius, and Marcus Aurelius—were capable, sophisticated rulers who expanded and solidified the empire, began or continued great building projects in Rome, and even tried to institute a few social reforms.

But all was not well with Rome as the reign of Marcus Aurelius (161–180 A.D.) drew to a close. The empire's boundaries had been stretched so far that the legions were kept constantly busy defending them against "barbarians" who failed to recognize the benefits of Roman rule and fought passionately to expel the invaders—from

LEFT: A troop of Praetorian Guards rides down "main street" of the Rome set, actually part of Malta's Fort Ricasoli. ABOVE: The Forum Romanum, an 1857 engraving by Johannes Heck, one of many images used as reference by the production.

39

ABOVE AND OPPOSITE: Production drawings by Denis Rich of the Imperial Palace interior and the square outside the Colosseum. BELOW: Cast members and extras in a Roman street scene.

Judea to the Scottish border, from the Danube to North Africa. Marcus Aurelius spent the better part of his time as emperor away from Rome, leading the legions against the Parthians, Germans, and Britons. Marcus probably was not too different from how he is depicted in the film: as a man more comfortable with the straightforward tasks, relationships, and perils of military life than with political intrigues back in Rome, and dangerously distanced from the people.

Communications in the far-flung empire were hugely difficult: a ruler could not be everywhere at once, as one could today, teleconferencing with the senate in Rome or with governors of distant provinces. His influence had to be maintained though instilling in local officials either a sense of personal loyalty and duty, or fear of Rome's military might. As Ridley Scott points out, "The empire probably just became too big to maintain."

What resources didn't go toward maintaining the armies mostly went into building and maintaining the Roman capital—the countryside was full of impoverished peasants tyrannized by rich landowners. Rural poverty plus the near-constant warfare in faraway lands resulted in massive immigration as peasants and vanquished

peoples streamed into Rome. The city became extremely overcrowded, and the majority of *plebs*—the poorest class—were unemployed, living off state-distributed food in a kind of welfare system. Nor had they any voice in politics. The gladiatorial games were one of several chief ways the emperors kept the idle masses occupied and diverted.

The city of Rome at this time was still near the peak of its physical magnificence, if starting to show signs of wear and tear. Most of Rome's great achievements in building roads, aqueducts, and great public edifices took place a little earlier, in the first century or before, though they still went on. The Forum was the center of public life, with its vast open spaces, speaker's platforms, statuary, and surrounding temples and basilicas. In the side streets, above a chaotic array of markets, shops and vendors, tenement dwellings up to seven stories high housed close to a million, while the wealthy built elegant one- and two-story villas (the *domus*). Roman breakthroughs in architectural engineering and durable building materials made all this possible, and it's why so much of ancient Rome still endures.

The emperors devoted as much effort to places of entertainment as to their halls of government and worship. The vast Circus Maximus, Rome's chariot-racing venue, was the empire's single largest structure; it no longer exists but the ruins of many theaters and amphitheaters ("round theater") do. And preeminent among these is the Colosseum, begun by the emperor Vespasian around 70 A.D. and completed by his son and heir Titus ten years later. Considered by some to be the greatest architectural feat of ancient Rome, it ironically was the setting for spectacles that showed Rome at its worst.

RIGHT: Set detail of a flambeau for the Colosseum, production drawing by Denis Rich.

THE CHARACTERS: REAL OR FICTION?

"Our history now plunges from a kingdom of gold to one of iron and rust." Thus did the Roman historian Dio Cassius describe what happened to Rome after Marcus Aurelius died and his son Commodus took power. *Gladiator* is a fictional story, though based on a real moment in history, and several of its main characters actually lived.

Marcus Aurelius (his full title was Imperator Caesar Marcus Aurelius Antoninus Augustus) was emperor from 161 to 180 A.D., and is portrayed by historians as wise, just, and competent. What isn't as well known (and the film doesn't mention) is that Marcus actually ruled as co-emperor with Lucius Verus, his adoptive brother and husband to his daughter Lucilla— although in practice Marcus was the real ruler.

As a youth Marcus adopted the Stoic philosophy, which emphasized virtues of duty, endurance, and self-sufficiency. Much of Marcus's reign indeed was spent waging war on the empire's borders. By contrast, he apparently held humanitarian principles and made efforts to aid the poor and political criminals. He did die on the Danubian frontier— probably from plague, though Commodus was with him at the time and hurried back to Rome shortly after, prompting speculation that he may have had a hand in his father's death.

In an odd reversal of history, Marcus in the film disinherits Commodus, planning to bestow his authority on the noble general Maximus. In fact, the real Marcus halted a practice followed by several emperors just preceding him: lacking sons, each had "adopted the ablest man available as his son, chief aide, and successor," writes one historian. "Marcus Aurelius ... reverted to the dynastic principle, designating his son Commodus as his successor despite his awareness of the young man's many shortcomings."

The Commodus of *Gladiator* is like the real man in some ways, unlike him in others. Certainly history has frowned on him in comparison with his father. But rather than the subtle, scheming, emotionally conflicted youth of the film, Commodus may simply have been not very bright, open to bad advice, and inclined to violent pleasures.

Commodus's passion for gladiatorial games and his own participation in them are well documented—he fought not only men but beasts, building a special platform from which he "hunted" in the arena. He sometimes decapitated ostriches on the run with crescent-shaped arrows, then implied to watching senators that he might do likewise to them.

At some point Commodus seems to have succumbed to megalomania. He took to dressing as the mythic hero Hercules in a lion skin and changed his name to Marcus Commodus Antoninus. His debaucheries became legendary; historian Aelius Lampridius says that "Commodus lived, rioting in the palace amid banquets and in baths along with 300 concubines. . . ."

THIS PAGE: Maximus, Marcus Aurelius, and Lucilla as portrayed in the film. OPPOSITE LEFT: Portrait bust of the Emperor Commodus in the guise of Hercules, c. 3rd century A.D., in the Museo del Palazzo dei Conservatori, Rome. Courtesy Scala/Art Resource, New York. RIGHT: Commodus in the film.

Commodus did not die in the arena, as in the film, but he *was* killed by an athlete. After many plots to assassinate him failed, in 192 A.D. he was strangled by a wrestler, apparently on the order of a Praetorian prefect (his mistress may also have been involved). In showing the dependence of Commodus on the powerful Praetorian Guard, the film strongly echoes history, for beginning with Commodus's reign, this elite military force acted as "kingmaker" to most emperors. In *Gladiator*, from almost the first scene to the last their presence is ominously felt.

Our hero Maximus was invented for the movie—but he does bear a resemblance to several historical figures. A general named Avidius Cassius was involved in the military campaign shown in the film and, on hearing a rumor of Marcus Aurelius's death, declared himself emperor but was assassinated by his own men. A more flattering comparison is with the emperor Diocletian, who ruled Rome from 284 to 305 A.D. Humbly born, like

Maximus, he became his emperor's trusted favorite and bodyguard, and later a general. Finally he was named heir and thus became emperor.

Other models might include Maximian, who co-ruled with Diocletian and was described as an able commander. The similarly named Maximin, emperor from 235-8 A.D., was "a rough Thracian soldier of great physical strength" who rose through the army ranks. Another close parallel is with the great soldier Trajan, the descendent of Roman settlers in Spain, whom the Emperor Nerva (96-8 A.D.) adopted and named his successor. At all events, there is plenty of precedent for the film's plot line of Marcus Aurelius adopting Maximus.

Commodus did in fact have a sister Lucilla, and she apparently hated her brother. Lucilla was at one time married to Lucius Verus, as her son tells Maximus in the film. (Again, there's no mention of Verus being co-emperor with Marcus.) Lucilla conspired against Commodus and tried to have him assassinated; in retaliation he banished her to the island of Capreae and later ordered her execution. So, unlike the film portrayal, Commodus actually outlived Lucilla.

43

THE GLADIATOR'S WORLD

"The people which once bestowed imperium, fasces, legions, everything, now has but two passionate desires: bread and circus games."

— JUVENAL

RIGHT AND OPPOSITE: Gladiator concept studies by Sylvain Despretz.

The poet Juvenal's famous lament about his compatriots' addiction to public spectacles was echoed by other educated Romans. But they were a distinct minority: by the time of Commodus's rule, gladiatorial games and chariot races were a major feature of Roman life. Some emperors, to solidify their own popularity and keep a largely unemployed populace diverted, decreed up to 150 consecutive days of games in the Colosseum or the Circus Maximus. To scholars and everyone else it remains a fascinating paradox that "a civilization so sophisticated and humane in many ways engaged in this consummate brutality," as Professor Andrew Wallace-Hadrill puts it.

Gladiatorial combat almost surely arose in the Etruscan era, just preceding the Roman period, as a part of funerary rites for the mighty. Essentially it was a human sacrifice: to win the gods' favor for the deceased (and not incidentally to entertain and impress the funeral

45

guests), combatants were forced to fight to the death. Along with other unsavory aspects of Etruscan culture, the Romans incorporated this practice into their own funeral games (which might also include nonlethal athletic contests). There is evidence of gladiator fights in Roman lands as early as the 3rd century B.C.

Typically for the Romans, more and bigger were always better. Soon powerful senators and equites (or knights, one of the ruling classes) were sponsoring gladiators and beast fights at other occasions: to mark a birthday, an anniversary, a military victory. The stakes kept rising: if one rich man put on a show with 20 gladiators, the next would make sure he had 30. Or if one brought in a crocodile, another would try for something even more exotic; say, a rhinoceros. And finally, when the emperors came to rule, they quickly observed what an effective public relations tool the games were and moved to monopolize the privilege of holding them. They would strictly control the scale of games produced by ordinary aristocrats so their own spectacles could stand out. "The games were absolutely at the center of the system of creating power," says Wallace-Hadrill. "They were called an offering, a gift by the emperor to his people."

The arena was the one place where the emperor and his people came into direct contact—and this is key to the games' enduring success. Here they were one, in a sense, enjoying the same drama, judging its effect and each others' reactions. "They're watching their emperors all the time," says Wallace-Hadrill, "they want to know what's the character of this guy. Is he a responsible sort who ought to be emperor or is he a beast? Some emperors got into trouble for taking manifest pleasure in seeing gladiators die."

Several different kinds of blood sports actually were held in the arena (the Roman word for "sand"), not all involving "gladiators" in the true sense. Mornings were usually devoted to beast fights, with professional hunters stalking and killing animals in a staged show, often with elab-

orate scenery suggesting the creature's native habitat. Or animals were made to fight each other: a bull against a bear, for instance. The noontime was reserved for the most horrific exhibitions, in which unarmed humans—perhaps war captives, criminals, or Christians—were simply sacrificed: executed by fully armed gladiators, forced to fight each other or be killed, mauled and devoured by wild animals, or dispatched in other creatively gruesome ways. Among Nero's most infamous deeds was turning Christians into torches—soaking their clothes with oil, crucifying them, and setting them alight in the arena.

The top-billed entertainers—the trained gladiators—were saved for last. Either in individual combat or large-scale spectacles that often restaged history (like the Battle of Carthage in the film), well-trained and heavily armed warriors fought with a variety of weapons—spear, sword, trident, dagger, mace, and more. An individual match might be fought to the death, or not, depending on the whim of the emperor and the cues he took from the crowd. If a man had fought especially well, or was a popular champion, he might be spared. Most in the audience were knowledgeable fans, familiar with individual fighters' styles and skills. Betting on the outcome was common.

Gladiators were slaves. To become one, you were either a slave already, or maybe a prisoner of war or a captive from a conquered land, or you signed your life away to a trainer/promoter like the film's Proximo. A career soldier like Maximus would never voluntarily become a gladiator; as Russell Crowe notes, "It's the bottom of the food chain as far as Max is concerned." It was also strictly taboo for anyone from the upper classes to fight as a gladiator—not that it didn't happen. A disgraced or poor younger son might choose the life, and even the powerful occasionally dared to enter the arena. The ultimate in flouting convention, of course, was when an emperor decided to be gladiator-for-a-day, as a few did—notably Commodus.

ABOVE: Gladiators train in the court-
yard of Proximo's compound, Rome
(Malta). BELOW: Concept study by
Sylvain Despretz.

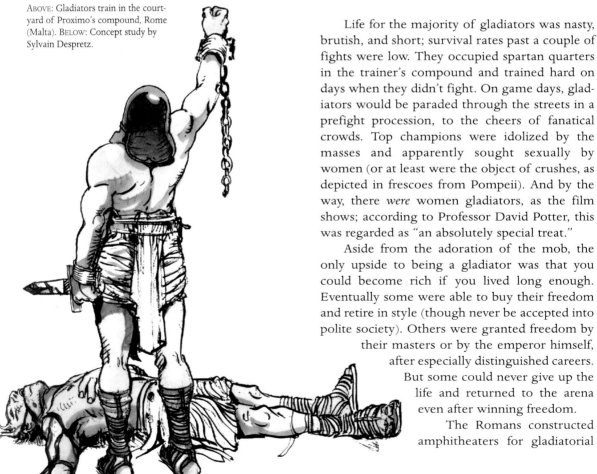

Life for the majority of gladiators was nasty, brutish, and short; survival rates past a couple of fights were low. They occupied spartan quarters in the trainer's compound and trained hard on days when they didn't fight. On game days, gladiators would be paraded through the streets in a prefight procession, to the cheers of fanatical crowds. Top champions were idolized by the masses and apparently sought sexually by women (or at least were the object of crushes, as depicted in frescoes from Pompeii). And by the way, there *were* women gladiators, as the film shows; according to Professor David Potter, this was regarded as "an absolutely special treat."

Aside from the adoration of the mob, the only upside to being a gladiator was that you could become rich if you lived long enough. Eventually some were able to buy their freedom and retire in style (though never be accepted into polite society). Others were granted freedom by their masters or by the emperor himself, after especially distinguished careers. But some could never give up the life and returned to the arena even after winning freedom.

The Romans constructed amphitheaters for gladiatorial

games in their conquered provinces, from France to Turkey. In some cases, when Romans tried to import gladiators, the local rulers and population were at first dismayed and revolted, but most eventually got used to it. The lesson, as Wallace-Hadrill points out, is that "any crowd can learn the excitement of watching men killing each other."

Inevitably, discussion of gladiators provokes comparisons with the violent sports today. Some claim that there's little real difference, that human nature has changed not at all, that given the right circumstances we too might cheer to watch contestants die. Others believe we're at least a bit more civilized—certainly we have better social and legal controls over our blood lust in sanctioned sports. It's hard to impose today's morality on Roman times, where mayhem and death were so ever-present in life through war, famine, and disease. "Could we be like them? Did they work differently as human beings?" asks Wallace-Hadrill. Who can know for sure?

ABOVE: The emperor's box with canopy, drawing by Arthur Max. RIGHT: Poster advertising "Wild-beast fights—150 days" in the Colosseum, created for the production by Jim Stanes. BELOW: Maximus and his fellow gladiators select the masks they will wear in combat.

SOLDIER, SENATOR, SOVEREIGN, SLAVE: CASTING *GLADIATOR*

The Romans, rulers, legionnaires, slaves, senators, and barbarian hordes who populate *Gladiator* are brought to life by a huge international cast. Ridley Scott was closely involved in selecting the principal actors, and the entire massive casting project was overseen by casting director Louis Digaimo. Casting duties in England were handled by Kathleen Mackie and Stephanie Corsalini; Billy Dowd is credited with gladiator and crowd casting.

For the leading roles, Scott and the producers sought actors who weren't necessarily box-office titans but who could believably convey the personalities and relationships in the story. Whoever played Maximus had to have the strength, gravity, and force to carry off a hero's part, and had to look convincing in his physical presence as a general and a gladiator. The portrayal of Commodus had to convey a subtle balance between malice and emotional turmoil; he couldn't be a standard villain. And for Lucilla, the filmmakers wanted not just a beautiful actress with a regal demeanor but one who could impart both intellectual strength and emotional vulnerability.

Gladiator's main cast includes several respected British veterans of the stage and screen, including Richard Harris as Emperor Marcus Aurelius, Derek Jacobi as Senator Gracchus, the late Oliver Reed as the gladiator trainer Proximo, and David Hemmings as the arena impresario Cassius. Russell Crowe laughingly referred to the quartet as "our four horsemen of the apocalypse."

"These actors are of a generation that experienced some of those earlier epics firsthand, particularly Richard," Scott says. "It was a thrill for me to have an opportunity to work with them, and all the more interesting to revisit the genre with them."

Russell Crowe as
MAXIMUS

The filmmakers knew that the actor chosen to play Maximus—the general-turned-gladiator whose popularity threatens the power of the emperor—was key to the success of the project. "It was crucial to find an actor who you could believe possessed the ferocity of this great warrior, but in whom you could also see a man of strong principle and character," affirms Douglas Wick. "Russell's name came up pretty fast. His intensity, his dignity, and his utter conviction in every role he undertakes made him everyone's first choice."

As Maximus, Crowe took on a very different challenge from his Oscar-nominated turn in *The Insider*. "He went from being a paunchy, middle-aged scientist to a gladiator—not bad," jokes Ridley Scott. "In other words, he's a real actor. Russell has an uncanny way of internalizing a role, and he's naturally very physical, which was a perfect combination for the part."

Crowe began his work on the part months before he even got a script to study: he had 45 pounds of extra weight, packed on for *The Insider*, to shed. For this he retreated to his ranch in Australia, where he worked outdoors with his livestock, watched his diet, and pursued a demanding exercise regimen that eventually included serious training in swordplay. He needed every minute of that conditioning, for once shooting began, his body took a near-daily beating as he battled Rome's enemies on the frontier and beasts and other gladiators in the arena. "I never really consider the day-to-day hardships I'm going to put myself through until I'm in the middle of it," Crowe says.

For Crowe, *Gladiator* offered the prospect of helping to re-establish a film genre while collaborating with a director he had long admired. "It was an extraordinary opportunity to work with one of the great visual artists of our time, and to

"This period is still fascinating to people—when you think of the amazing achievements of the Roman Empire, yet underscored by absolute brutality."

—RUSSELL CROWE

play a character who undergoes such a remarkable journey," he says. "Maximus goes from being a great general to being shackled and sold into slavery as a gladiator—a slight change in lifestyle," he smiles. "For a while then he lives only to stand in front of the new emperor and exact his revenge, but he is caught up in the political turmoil of the day and can't help but become involved. For want of a better expression, he's a good man."

Connie Nielsen as
LUCILLA

Daughter of Marcus Aurelius and sister of the new emperor Commodus, Lucilla is played by Danish-born actress Connie Nielsen. "We spent a long time looking for the right actress to play Lucilla," recalls producer Branko Lustig. "When we saw Connie, we knew we had found her. I had the feeling I was watching a young Sophia Loren in *The Fall of the Roman Empire*. She is a wonderful actress and had the presence we needed in Lucilla."

The script completely gripped me," Nielsen offers. "There are colossal elements, like the setting and the battles, and yet the story is very intimate in how it brings you into the personal relationships between people, especially in the case of Lucilla. She is caught between the ambitions of her brother and the will of Maximus, with whom she has a past.

"It's interesting that we generate a lot of history between Maximus and Lucilla without ever going into it," Ridley Scott expounds. "We gather it was a romance that went wrong, but I like

that exactly what happened between them remains obscure."

Nielsen also was fascinated by Lucilla's ability to operate within the mores of her day. "She lives in a time when women did not have a voice, at least officially," she notes. "But she is her father's daughter and has been raised in the center of much political intrigue, so she is definitely capable of using whatever is at her disposal to survive."

"In many ways she loves her brother, but she is also fearful of him and even more afraid of the power he holds over her son, Lucius."

Joaquin Phoenix as
COMMODUS

The man upon whom Maximus seeks his revenge is Commodus, who becomes emperor of Rome upon the death of Marcus Aurelius. It was important to the drama that Maximus's strength be counterbalanced by an equal measure of power on the part of his adversary—albeit a different kind of power. The filmmakers found what they were looking for in the quiet intensity of Joaquin Phoenix.

Ridley Scott had earlier worked with Phoenix when he executive produced the film *Clay Pigeons*, in which the actor starred. "When we offered him the part, I think the most surprised person was Joaquin himself," the director says. "He is not the physically imposing type one might have envisioned in the role, but he conveys the complexities of this corrupt ruler in a very courageous way. He exposes the vulnerability that is juxtaposed with the ruthlessness of Commodus."

The mercurial quality of the part was one of the incentives for Phoenix, along with the chance to work with Scott and a distinguished group of actors on a movie of such spectacle and scope. "Commodus is a character I really enjoyed exploring," Phoenix reflects. "I think the best way to describe him is as a spoiled child. He's 19 years old but wields an incredible amount of power—so he has all the emotions that go with being that age without having had the guidance he needed to handle that power. He's vulnerable and sad one minute and throwing a tantrum the next. He desperately wants the love of the people, but the irony of the story is that the gladiatorial games he decrees to get the masses to love him are ultimately what bring his nemesis to Rome."

"This is an epic but also a very character-driven story. That's what was exciting about it for me."

—JOAQUIN PHOENIX

55

Oliver Reed as
PROXIMO

The closing credits of *Gladiator* bear a dedication to "our friend, Oliver Reed," because the 61-year-old actor died during the filming in Malta, ending a career that was nearly as famous for hard living and scrapping as for the superb performances Reed generated in film after film. Before that shocking event—which occurred after Reed had completed most but not all of his scenes—the actor spoke with humor and enthusiasm about working on the production.

Reed's performance as Proximo, the tough and cynical trainer of gladiators, is among the film's highlights; one reviewer wrote that it was a treat just to watch Proximo raise his eyebrows while observing Maximus fight. "I'm a gladiator trainer who in the past was a gladiator himself, and who won his freedom," Reed explains. "I'm responsible for finding out if Maximus can fight, taking him to Rome, and putting him into the big game. Proximo's a wonderful character—but then, if you're involved in something this big, you have to believe that your character can compete with everything else that's going on."

Reed researched his part by viewing documentaries on Roman times, "and the first thing I did was look at the hairstyles." But for the most part, he says, "an actor is only as good as the script he eventually gets. You can look at old statues and paintings from Pompeii—but the rest is in the script and the way the director uses his camera."

Ironically, the character of Proximo dies in one of the film's last scenes, after giving Maximus his chance to escape. Reed, who spoke admiringly of the technological accomplishments on *Gladiator*, might have been glad to know that the few missing frames in his swansong performance were filled in through the wonders of CGI.

"Occasionally some filmmaker comes up with an idea that interests me—and this was certainly one of those occasions."

Derek Jacobi as
GRACCHUS

"I've worn a lot of togas in my time," recalls the distinguished actor Derek Jacobi—and anyone who saw his landmark performance in the title role of the BBC's *I, Claudius* knows that few actors have worn them any better. In *Gladiator* he plays Gracchus, the "rather posh senator" who is determined to end the corrupt reign of Commodus, even at the risk of his own life and many others.

After a long, brilliant career on stage and screen, in which he has won many honors including a knighthood, Jacobi still approaches each role as a fresh challenge. And, he adds, "when Ridley Scott says, 'I've got a part for you in my movie,' you don't say no, do you?" Jacobi enjoys the contrast between live theater and film work, and appreciates the massive effort that went into making *Gladiator* as real as possible. "Unlike on a stage, where you have to suspend your disbelief, this is almost like the real thing. You respond to the size of it all in your performance."

"I love this period, for a start. And I love that

"Unlike on a stage, where you have to suspend your disbelief, this is almost like the real thing. You respond to the size of it all in your performance."

the film is dealing with people and relationships in this incredibly exciting setting. The best sorts of epic films, I think were about people—look at *Gone With the Wind*. People in a great saga, a huge narrative—that's what's exciting."

He also enjoyed working and hanging with his compatriots, Richard Harris, Oliver Reed, and David Hemmings. "We all knew about each other but had never met—when it happened here, we sort of became instant friends. We were constantly encouraging each other and laughing a great deal. I think that sometimes worries American actors: the way English actors giggle all the time and seem to be taking things very lightly. In fact, we take them just as seriously, but the humor always kicks in."

Djimon Hounsou as
JUBA

"In his mind, he is with his people; his loved ones are there, waiting for him. That ability to find freedom in his mind is something he tries to share with Maximus."

After Maximus is kidnapped into slavery, he finds a friend and companion in the Numidian named Juba, a fellow captive and gladiator. Juba is portrayed by the young actor Djimon Hounsou, from Senegal by way of France, who made a big impression in his first starring role as the African captive Cinque in Steven Spielberg's *Amistad*. So it's not surprising that the DreamWorks filmmakers thought of him when casting Juba.

It's always hard for an actor to choose his or her follow-up roles after a spectacular start like *Amistad*, and this was much on Hounsou's mind in thinking about *Gladiator*. In fact, he was troubled by the frequency of the "slave" references in earlier versions of the script, and worked with the writers and producers to broaden the conception of Juba's character.

But doing the film was great fun, he says. "This is a boy's dream, you know—to come and play gladiators, be a tough boy. And when you look around at these sets, and the crowds, it's so real that it's easy to bring the emotions out, to be there as a gladiator. Especially the first few times, when the chariots race in and come straight toward you—it's impressive!"

Juba and Maximus form a deep bond by sav-ing each other's lives, but their relationship has a spiritual component too, based on their cultures' belief in an afterlife. Juba survives his ordeal by looking forward to reunion with his beloved family, and he manages to pass that comfort on to Maximus. "Juba is a very skillful fighter, which enables him to stay alive physically, but he knows a way to stay alive mentally and spiritually as well. In his mind, he is with his people; his loved ones are there, waiting for him."

Richard Harris as
MARCUS AURELIUS

Legendary actor Richard Harris gave *Gladiator* its strongest link with the past of Roman-era spectacles on film. Back in the early 1960s, when Anthony Mann was casting *The Fall of the Roman Empire*, Harris was originally signed to play the role of Commodus. Marcus Aurelius was played by the great Alec Guinness. But the famously hot-tempered Harris "got in a big row with the director . . . there were rewrites, and then I walked out of it," leaving Christopher Plummer to take over his part. Now, nearly 40 years later, Harris steps into the role of the ailing Marcus and informs it with his questing face and arresting voice.

"It was a smashing part for me," Harris declares. "Marcus is a man in crisis, wrestling with demons. He was a scholar and a philosopher, but he spent 16 of his 20 years as emperor fighting battles and spilling blood to expand the empire. Now nearing the end, he comes to realize that his life has been a fraud, and that he has actually ruined his children—especially Commodus."

"Modern audiences have never been exposed to an epic movie on this subject, not since Spartacus. *So there's a real opportunity here to show the public a part of our history."*

For the past ten years, Harris has sworn that each film he makes will be his last, but when Ridley Scott came calling he couldn't resist. "When you're working with a guy like Ridley," says Harris, "you just put yourself in his hands." Harris would often sit with Scott on the set as the director explained the mechanics of making action epics today—how the total effect of stupendous sets and countless extras would later be augmented with computer work—much to the actor's wonderment. "Every time I'm on a movie set, I'm still in awe," says Harris. "Especially this . . . the size of it. I can't help but think, 'How did you do this? How did you marshall it all in your imagination?'"

ABOVE: A ruined casbah in Tamdahkt, Morocco. OPPOSITE TOP: Production still photo of a North African caravan. RIGHT: A Roman gate and city street from Volubilis, the empire's westernmost settlements in North Africa. The well-preserved ruins at Volubilis date from the first century and include a forum, temple, basilica, and mansions, one containing an elaborate floor mosaic. Volubilis and other provincial towns were often governed by retired legionnaires whose principal job was maintaining control over local populations. Location photos by Arthur Max.

SURVEYING AN EMPIRE

The story that emerged from development ranged over a substantial chunk of the ancient Roman Empire—from the forests of Germania to the deserts of North Africa to the heart of Rome itself. One of the earliest logistical challenges was to determine where these settings would be re-created.

It was soon clear that the production would travel—a lot. "The movie is very big, of course," points out producer Branko Lustig, who handled most of the line-producing details on *Gladiator*. "And if we hadn't done it on location—if we had to construct everything on soundstages in Los Angeles—the cost of the movie would have been double or triple."

Originally the filmmakers concentrated on scouting sites that contained ruins of the Empire, both to soak up atmosphere and to learn whether any of them could serve as filming locations. "We tromped around the Roman Empire for six weeks," says production designer Arthur Max, "scouting all the existing remains in England, France, Italy, eastern Europe, and North Africa. We looked at the

ruins, the museum collections, tried to get a flavor for what it really was like.

"But the empire was, at least as we imagined, a much more fantastic place than you can tell from looking at the remnants. Your access to what's left of the real Rome is quite limited. All the ruins are historical monuments, and so cannot be touched. They were very interesting for reference but unusable for our purpose—the stunt work we would have to do, for example, or the crowd work. And so we went in search of a living world, not an archaic, museum world."

Their search led them all over Europe and the Mediterranean. For the film's early sequences, featuring an enormous battle between Roman legions and Germanic tribes, the filmmakers first planned to shoot at an army base outside Bratislava, the ancient capital of the Slovak Republic. A port on the Danube, Bratislava isn't far from where Marcus Aurelius and his legions actually campaigned. But the schedule was pushed forward and winter was approaching, raising concern that too much snow in Slovakia might hamper progress. Then Ridley Scott had the practical notion of starting the production odyssey closer to home: not far from London, in fact. Scott says, "I figured, we're starting a big movie, and to move the entire unit to Slovakia to be in pine trees . . . well, I may as well be in pine trees in England, frankly, and save that horrible first month, where everybody's worried about the hotel and their laundry while you're trying to do this massive thing." So the Germania sequences ended up being filmed in a forest near Farnham, in Surrey.

After Maximus is enslaved, he is brought in chains to North Africa, where Proximo is buying prospective new gladiators and training them to

"We tromped around the Roman Empire for six weeks scouting all the existing remains in England, France, Italy, Eastern Europe, and North Africa. We looked at the ruins, the museum collections, tried to get a flavor for what it really was like."

—Production Designer Arthur Max

ABOVE: The ancient casbah and citadel of Ait Ben Haddou, Morocco, where most of the North African scenes were filmed. Photo panorama by Arthur Max. BELOW: The forest in Farnham, England, that became the site for the Germania battle. Photo by John Nelson.

fight at a small provincial arena. To film these scenes, the production went to Ouarzazate, Morocco. "This was a place Ridley knew about from previous scouting," says Arthur Max, "and it really was magic. I mean, exotic, romantic. It's an ancient citadel town with the Atlas Mountains as a backdrop, and Morocco's oldest existing casbah nearby."

And, finally, Rome. Another of Ridley Scott's films, *White Squall*, had taken him to Malta—an island republic in the central Mediterranean, off the southern tip of Sicily and east of Tunisia. Known as the "fortress island," Malta holds pre-Phoenician ruins up to 6,000 years old and became part of the Roman Empire in 218 B.C. On his previous trip, Scott had noted the remains of historic Fort Ricasoli, a 17th-century Spanish fort later converted to a barracks by Napoleon's invading forces. When Arthur Max accompanied Scott to scout the fort, both were convinced this was the ideal place to recreate the center of ancient Rome and its splendid Colosseum.

ROME WASN'T
REBUILT IN A DAY

Spanning three seasons and four countries, production on *Gladiator* presented the filmmakers with any number of logistical hurdles to overcome. Branko Lustig remarks, "In many ways, it was like making four different movies because we had to coordinate the efforts of four separate crews: one in London, one in Malta, one in Morocco, and one central crew that moved from location to location."

Verisimilitude became the hallmark of the entire production, though Scott was determined that *Gladiator* never be seen as a page out of a history book. "There is a great deal written about the Roman Empire, but there are also questions about what is accurate and what is merely conjecture. I felt the priority was to stay true to the spirit of the period, but not necessarily to adhere to facts. We were, after all, creating fiction, not practicing archaeology."

Scott continues, "The most important thing when you assume a challenge like this is choosing the right people to work with, because you have no choice but to delegate on a production this size. I had the best department heads—people who had been there, seen it, done it, or researched it. I knew I could rely on their artistry to craft the world in which our story unfolds, and they did an extraordinary job."

In creating the world of *Gladiator*, Scott's chief lieutenant was production designer Arthur Max, who was responsible for conceptualizing the entire visual side of the film and supervising its execution. Max had earlier designed *G.I. Jane* for Scott and also was the production designer on

Spring, by Lawrence Alma-Tadema, 1894. Courtesy the J. Paul Getty Museum. The painting depicts a procession of servants of the Temple of Flora celebrating the Roman festival of Cereralia. Alma-Tadema's images were a major source of reference for the *Gladiator* production, and also served as inspiration for C. B. DeMille's 1934 *Cleopatra* and other films.

ABOVE: Proximo's provincial gladiator school in Morocco.
LEFT: Early morning in the Roman market square set, Malta.
Photo by John Nelson.

David Fincher's dark thriller *Seven*. Prior to becoming a production designer, Max worked as an art director on Nicholas Roeg's *Insignificance* and Hugh Hudson's *Revolution*, and an assistant art director on *Cal*.

"The chief problem for me," says Max, "was how to achieve the scale demanded by this film—not only the size of Rome itself and the Colosseum, but to convey a sense of the vastness of the empire beyond Rome. For this production," he smiles, "size matters."

Because of the far-flung locations, working on *Gladiator* was "really like trying to design four movies at the same time." Max engaged trusted art directors who oversaw separate production design departments in each major location, while he traveled back and forth among them. Each department had its own staff of set decorators, stylists, prop buyers, construction workers, costume and wardrobe staff, and more. "What I'm most proud of on this production is the incredible teamwork in my department, and the way they interpreted my designs," says Max.

But Max's work began far in advance of production, climbing a mountain of research and consulting extensively with Scott to achieve the look they wanted in every detail. "There's an overwhelming amount of information—the problem is to be selective, to discover what's relevant to what you're doing, and what's fresh." Paintings were an important source of visual inspiration to Scott and Max. "We started pinning pictures on the wall, grabbing references and images from all over, and sort of collaging our way forward," Max recalls. "That would stimulate our dialogue and help set the directions we wanted to go in.

"We tried to bring to *Gladiator* a sense of the Roman Empire in decline—its greatness and at the same time its corruption and decay. And to do that we found ourselves looking not so much to the scholarly historical realm as to interpretations of Rome by certain 19th-century painters— classical Romantics who depicted an exotic view of Rome as they wished it to be, not as it really was. We tried to be relatively faithful to history, but we wanted to visually dramatize our subject, make it as exciting, as rich and baroque as we possibly could. And so it's a very eclectic interpretation of the Roman Empire."

Not only was *Gladiator* shot in four locations, but in each place all the sets, props, and costumes were custom-made for the film. "Everything you see was made by us," says Branko Lustig. "To rent what we needed would have been prohibitively expensive, or it wasn't readily available. So we made our own costumes, weaponry, and armor; built our own chariots and wagons; constructed all the sets—except in cases where we added to existing buildings, as in Malta."

ABOVE: Production designer Arthur Max on the set in Malta. Photo by Sylvain Despretz. LEFT: Concept sketch of the Rome set by Ridley Scott. BELOW LEFT: The Rome set with the equestrian statue of Marcus Aurelius, sculpted for the production by John Robinson. Photo by John Nelson. BELOW RIGHT: Ancient Roman archway, architectural rendering by Adam O'Neill.

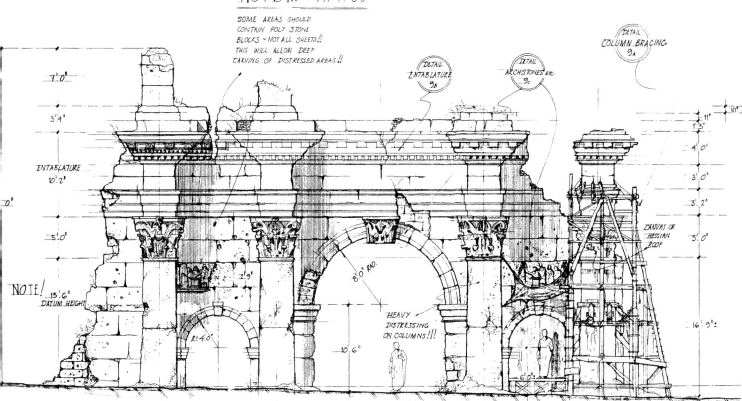

*NOTE!!! 11.1.'99

SOME AREAS SHOULD
CONTAIN POLY STONE
BLOCKS ~ NOT ALL SHEETS!!
THIS WILL ALLOW DEEP
CARVING OF DISTRESSED AREAS!!

GERMANIA (ENGLAND)

Principal photography on *Gladiator* got under way in a forest in Farnham, England, which doubled for Germania—a vast swath of eastern and northern Europe peopled by many tribes, all hostile to the Roman occupiers. As a production challenge, this segment of location filming had it all: difficult terrain; winter weather; thousands of extras to train, costume, and equip; exotic period weaponry to construct; sweeping battle panoramas to choreograph and capture; and to top it all off, a fiery conflagration in which a large chunk of forest burned to the ground.

The Romans' technology gave them a big advantage over their barbarian foes, and the film went to great lengths to design and build war machines similar to what the legions would have used. In the Germania battle, before the Roman infantry advances, archers fire thousands of flaming arrows and the artillery launches earthen pots full of oil from huge catapults. While the pots are airborne, giant mechanized crossbows called "scorpions" fire flaming bolts that pierce the pots, raining fire onto the terrified enemy—and of course setting the woods on fire. This wasn't a problem: one reason the Farnham site was chosen was that the filmmakers had learned from England's Forestry Commission that the area (known as Bourne Woods) was slated to be deforested anyway. "So I said, 'I'll do it. I'll burn it to the ground,'" recounts Ridley Scott. "They said, 'Good.'"

Arthur Max recalls, "Our biggest challenge was creating all the specialized equipment. Almost everything had to be made from scratch, and it had to actually work. The other challenge was the weather, as we were building mid-winter in a muddy site full of holes, trying to paint and age our sets in driving, horizontal freezing rain." He adds wryly, "Other than that it was very simple."

In the battle, 5,000 legionnaires take on some 10,000 Germanic tribesmen. While not quite that many were mustered for the film, several thousand extras and stuntmen enacted plenty of superb battle footage, their numbers later augmented with CG effects. Another small army of costumers, armorers, fight trainers, makeup artists, hairdressers, and prosthetics technicians saw to it that the combatants were convincingly arrayed, equipped, and schooled in fighting with sword and spear; then muddied, bloodied, or maimed as the action called for. Several animal handlers were kept busy, too, making sure that the dramatic cavalry charge led by Maximus was heartstopping yet caused the horses no harm.

Once filming started, the weather cooperated splendidly. "I was expecting the worst," says Scott, "the usual English weather: snow, sleet, rain, filth, mud. . . . But for nearly a month while

ABOVE: The Roman legions and their war machines (note catapults at far left) prepare for battle. BELOW: Snow (real and special-effects) falls during the Germania battle scene.

we were shooting I got brilliant weather, temperate, maybe 50 degrees. Cold enough to show your breath. Not too much rain. Perfect ground, and we moved like lightning."

An incident that took place in Farnham convinced Russell Crowe that *Gladiator* had great karma attached to it. Written into the script was a moment when General Maximus, about to lead his legions into battle, looks up to the sky, sniffs the winter air, and predicts, "Snow." Crowe was dubious of turning Maximus into a weatherman with so much else on his mind, though of course the moviemakers could manufacture snow whenever they needed. But just 10 minutes before take one of the battle sequence—which they had spent days setting up—snow actually began falling in the Surrey forest. "So suddenly Max is not only a great general but also the only reliable weatherman in history," laughs Crowe. "I mean, that kind of magic just doesn't happen, but it happened all along on this film."

Charge of the Felix cavalry,
production drawing by Sylvain
Despretz. Inset photo shows
the same scene as it was filmed,
complete with special-effects
explosions and flames.

72

NUMIDIA (Morocco)

Proximo's market square, drawing by supervising art director (Morocco) Benjamin Fernandez. OPPOSITE BELOW: The citadel of Ait Ben Haddou, showing the provincial amphitheater set built for the production.

From England, the company moved to Ouarzazate, Morocco—which offered the perfect setting to create the marketplace where Maximus is sold, Proximo's gladiator school, and the small arena in which Maximus and Juba get their first taste of gladiatorial combat. Just outside Ouarzazate is the oldest casbah in the world, which is known to have stood for about 500 years but whose foundations probably date back to Roman times.

"In some ways, Morocco designed itself," marvels Arthur Max. "You come up over a hill and you're in another time. It was extraordinary to find this ancient casbah, and, conveniently enough, there was an empty field at the base of the town where the locals played football. It was the ideal spot for us to erect a small, provincial arena where our hero is introduced to the gladiator's life."

The newly built amphitheater had to be indistinguishable from the ancient architecture surrounding it. So the construction team, supervised by Spanish art director Benjamin Fernandez, used only indigenous materials and local methods practiced for generations to manufacture 30,000 mud bricks for the structure. "The bricks were made of simple mud, mixed with straw, cast in a mold and baked in the sun," says Max. "When the arena took shape on the landscape, it looked like it had been there for centuries."

The production also employed local citizens as extras in the arena and in the bazaar, where both slaves and animals were purchased. As befit the setting, the weathered faces of the Moroccans gave no hint that they would return to the 20th century when Ridley Scott called "cut."

Three views of the provincial arena at Ait Ben Haddou: ABOVE, in a concept drawing by Benjamin Fernandez; LEFT: under construction; and OPPOSITE, during the filming of the chain fight scene.

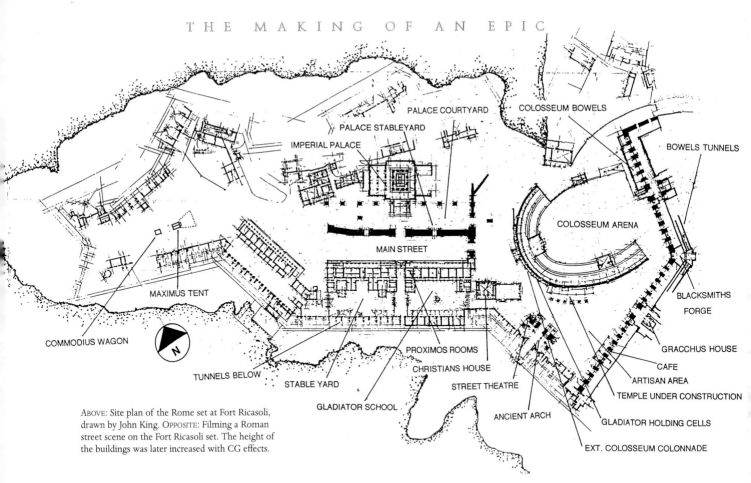

PALACE COURTYARD
COLOSSEUM BOWELS
PALACE STABLEYARD
IMPERIAL PALACE
BOWELS TUNNELS
COLOSSEUM ARENA
MAIN STREET
MAXIMUS TENT
BLACKSMITHS FORGE
COMMODIUS WAGON
N
GRACCHUS HOUSE
PROXIMOS ROOMS
CAFE
CHRISTIANS HOUSE
ARTISAN AREA
TUNNELS BELOW
STABLE YARD
STREET THEATRE
TEMPLE UNDER CONSTRUCTION
GLADIATOR SCHOOL
ANCIENT ARCH
GLADIATOR HOLDING CELLS
EXT. COLOSSEUM COLONNADE

ABOVE: Site plan of the Rome set at Fort Ricasoli, drawn by John King. OPPOSITE: Filming a Roman street scene on the Fort Ricasoli set. The height of the buildings was later increased with CG effects.

ROME (Malta)

On the "fortress island" of Malta, the production took on its greatest challenge yet: recreating the center of Rome—encompassing the Forum and the Colosseum—the geographic and political heart of the Empire. Arthur Max had an invaluable head start on research for this crucial aspect of the production. "I had the advantage of having lived and worked in Rome and done some of my architectural training there. I knew the actual locations firsthand."

Max went with Scott to scout the Malta location, Port Mifisalfi, which contained the sprawling, abandoned barracks of Fort Ricasoli. Scott recalls, "Essentially, it was an English barracks from 1803—they had built an extensive complex out of beautiful yellow limestone in the Romanesque style. Giant vaulted walls, hollow inside, with gun emplacements for huge cannons.

You're talking about big architecture, which the prevailing wind in Malta and the blowing sand had nicely aged. So it looked like ancient Rome.

"There was also a giant parade ground," Scott adds, "that would fit our Colosseum perfectly. Arthur and I figured that the existing buildings had already provided some of the pieces, so if we integrated our sets with the real thing, we'd complete a fantastic jigsaw puzzle." And that's what they did, with existing structures providing about half the final sets seen on film.

In addition to the Colosseum, the Fort Ricasoli compound held the physical sets for the emperor's palace, the Forum, the senate antechamber, the Roman marketplace, and the residence of Senator Gracchus. Ridley Scott estimated that the Fort Ricasoli location gave him about $5 million of instant production value.

Again, Scott used paintings to capture the spirit of the environment he was striving to create. Other influences for Rome were the modernist architecture of Hugh Ferriss and the oppressive statements of power created by Nazi-era architects like Albert Speer, with their imperial references. "Ridley definitely wanted to capture a concept of Rome as the New York City of its day, an overwhelming environment and a monument to itself," says visual effects supervisor John Nelson.

Max outlines the design process for the Rome sets: "We photographed and measured the location, then built a large-scale model of all the existing buildings in block form—very rough, just to get an idea of what was there. Then we started constructing building blocks: bits of wall, bits of building, a few temples, the basic essentials of any ancient Rome set. We photographed those from various angles using a miniature video camera, and then video-printed them.

"The next step was drawing those elements specifically for the movie, using renderings by production illustrator Denis Rich. When we were happy with those concepts and had tried juggling them around, we finally went to technical working drawings for construction purposes. As a final track, we plotted the working designs into a computer and printed them as three-dimensional renderings, including lighting, shade, and color, showing certain angles and what we would receive through the camera. This was partly to make sure that we had enough practical set to build on later with CGI."

Over a period of 19 weeks, more than 100 British technicians and 200 Maltese tradespeople labored to build the sets, overlaying ancient Rome onto 19th-century Malta. Their efforts were constantly hampered by high winds and storms in what was reported to be Malta's worst winter in 30 years. Something like 600 tons of plaster were used in the sets, by Max's recollection; the production went through all the plaster and plywood in Malta and had to start shipping it in. "Sometimes the ships bringing equipment or supplies couldn't dock because of the storms."

Roman market square with Port Mifisalfi in the background. In the foreground is the giant foot sculpted by John Robinson—what the production needed to show of a colossal statue of the Emperor Nero.

THE COLOSSEUM

Gladiator's supreme production challenge was recreating Rome's Colosseum—the greatest architectural expression of Rome's power and still the most impressive of its surviving monuments. The filmmakers steeped themselves in history, architecture, and engineering to equip themselves for the task.

The Colosseum is the largest of all ancient amphitheaters—a uniquely Roman building type created by joining two theaters at their open ends so the auditorium completely surrounds an elliptical arena, lined with sand to absorb blood. The direct descendants of Roman arenas are Spain's bull rings, and the moviemakers looked at a few of these as possible location candidates. Amphitheaters like the Colosseum were built especially for blood sports, which formerly had been held in circuses, forums, and other public buildings—but this proved dangerous for spectators, leading in one case to elephants stampeding into the crowd. The Colosseum's builders took care to place the lowest seats well above the killing ground; animals were kept securely caged in underground cells.

Rome had had a few smaller amphitheaters since early imperial times, but nothing like this. Begun by the emperor Vespasian in 70 A.D. and inaugurated by his son Titus about a decade later, the Colosseum arose on the site of a one-time lake at the foot of the Esquiline hill—part of the emperor Nero's Golden House, a magnificent palace and park complex. The name "Colosseum" comes from a colossal statue of Nero that once stood nearby. (Just its foot appears in the film.) The amphitheater was an extravagant gift by the emperor to the Roman people, restoring to public use a chunk of central real estate that Nero had commandeered for his private property. Not incidentally, erecting such a wondrous building in only a decade helped the new Flavian dynasty make a massive impression.

81

Nero's Rome was dotted with artificial lakes he had created in order to stage one of his favorite entertainments: mock naval battles. Because the Colosseum was built on a filled-in natural lake, elaborate drainage systems had to be designed. And some historians believe (though others disagree) that in the amphitheater's early days, the arena was occasionally flooded for staging such watery warfare. In any case, after the next emperor, Domitian, added a subterranean network of corridors, this wouldn't have been possible. (The Colosseum's huge drains, by the way, have provided superb archaeological evidence of what Roman spectators wore, brought to, and ate at the games.)

The Colosseum was an utter marvel of design, construction, and engineering for its time, or any time. The Romans' mastery of the arch and their invention of superior concrete-wall construction enabled the Colosseum to rise a lofty four stories high. The lower three tiers are a series of giant stacked arcades, each featuring columns in the Greek "orders": from bottom to top, Ionic, Doric, and Corinthian. These columns are decorative; the real structural units are the massive arch-bearing piers. The top story, instead of an arcade, is a smooth wall decorated with square columns (pilasters) and projecting corbels,

PRECEDING PAGES: Exterior of the Colosseum set under construction. The production built only a portion of the first tier to scale. From the outside, the real Colosseum is a giant ellipse measuring 620 by 500 feet; its interior arena was 290 by 180 feet. RIGHT: Elevation view of the Colosseum main gate, drawn by Peter Russell. OPPOSITE: Progressive stages in the building of the Colosseum set, as seen from the Fort Ricasoli ramparts. Working on a sloping site, the crew had to install foundations that actually raised the ground level about six feet, then backfilled with gravel and stone rubble, which was later capped with sand. Photos by Helen Xenopoulos.

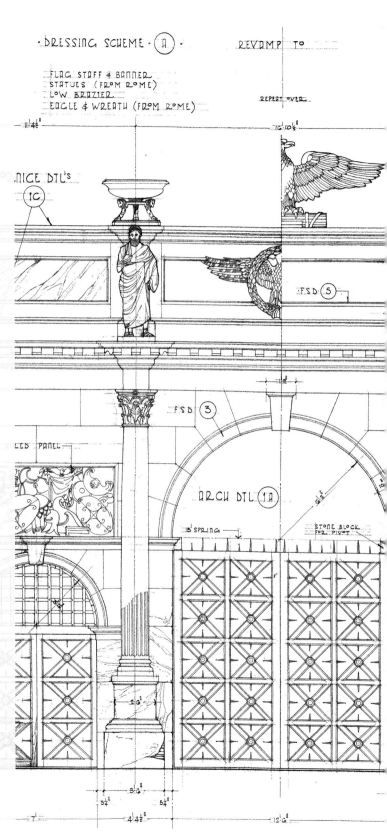

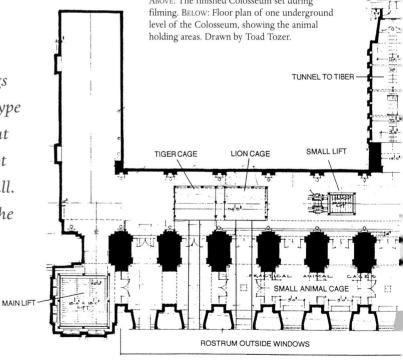

ABOVE: The finished Colosseum set during filming. BELOW: Floor plan of one underground level of the Colosseum, showing the animal holding areas. Drawn by Toad Tozer.

TUNNEL TO TIBER

TIGER CAGE   LION CAGE   SMALL LIFT

SMALL ANIMAL CAGE

MAIN LIFT

ROSTRUM OUTSIDE WINDOWS

"We started looking at bull rings because the bull ring is the archetype of the ancient Roman arena. But most of those we found were not usable because they were too small. They didn't have the scale that the actual Colosseum had."

—ARTHUR MAX

which supported masts for rigging the velarium—a huge canvas awning drawn over the auditorium for shade. The exterior was faced with Travertine marble, thousands of tons of it brought by wagon from far-off quarries. The arcades were filled with statuary; the passageways lavishly gilded.

The interior structure is no less marvelous, with its four tiers of seating reared one upon the other, and its complex system of passageways and stairs. It was designed so that spectators came in by a particular entrance, then were channeled via a series of interlaced corridors and stairways, to emerge exactly at their designated seating area. All the seats had good views of the arena floor—something modern stadium-builders don't always achieve! The vault (a kind of arch set sideways) was another Roman architectural breakthrough used extensively throughout the Colosseum, in barrel-vaulted corridors joined at cross-vaulted intersections.

Below the wooden arena floor lay a hidden, dimly lit maze of corridors, shafts, hand-winched elevators, staging areas for sets and props, and holding pens for gladiators, victims, and animals. Ramps led upward to two main portals—on one of the amphitheater's long sides was an entrance, the door of life; on the other, an exit, the door of death. Other entrances were made through trap doors in the arena floor; for instance, those of the wild beasts, whose pens were cleverly designed on two levels. When showtime arrived, slaves hoisted up the animals in open-ended cages from the lower to the upper level, which opened in front onto a ramp. The desperate animals ran up the ramp seeking freedom, straight through a trap door into the arena to kill or be killed.

Outside and nearby the Colosseum was at least one gladiator training school, as well as armories, scenery shops, a hospital for the wounded, and burial pits where corpses, human and animal, were disposed of. The ground-floor

BELOW: Maximus ascends the ramp to the arena.

EXISTING WORKSHOP

TUNNEL TO ARENA

ABOVE LEFT: Ridley Scott with a model of the Colosseum set built by senior prop maker Roland Stevenson. ABOVE RIGHT: Storyboard drawings by Sylvain Despretz of the Colosseum exterior and interior, made for CGI studies. RIGHT: Digital photograph of the overhead "blimp shot" created by VFX, which passes over the city and the top of the Colosseum, showing the crowd of 33,000 computer-generated spectators in the stands. Photo Mill Film Ltd. BELOW: Elevation view of the interior Colosseum set, drawn by Peter Russell.

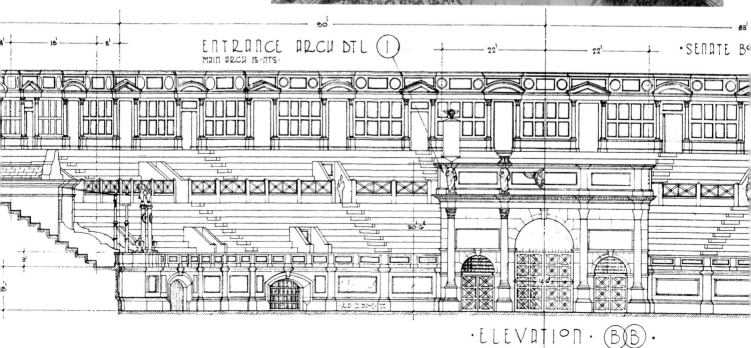

ENTRANCE ARCH DTL ①
MAIN ARCH IS NTS.

· SENATE B·

· ELEVATION · BB

ABOVE: View of the back of the Colosseum set from the parapet wall of Fort Ricasoli (foreground), looking down on the market square set and a temple under construction. The valerium panels used for filming are seen at the top of the Colosseum set. Photo by Sylvain Despretz.

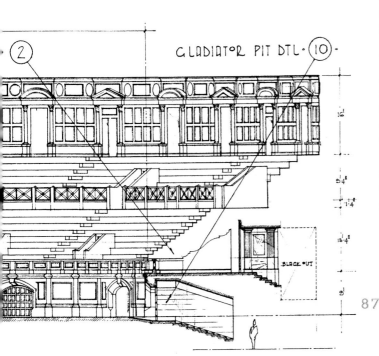

arcade of the building was crowded on game days with bookmakers and vendors selling everything from snacks to programs to seat cushions to gladiator dolls (the action figures of the day). Inside the building, hundreds more worked to put on the shows and keep the crowds happy: the slaves below ground, the hawkers in the stands, the attendants who sprinkled scented water (to mask the smell of blood), the riggers who opened and closed the velarium, the umpires who supervised matches, and the *incitators* in the ring, brandishing whips or hot irons to enforce their commands to "strike" or "slay"!

Early on, the filmmakers debated how to realize the Colosseum on screen: Could it be a real location? Would they have to build the entire amphitheater from scratch? Would it have to be done entirely in CGI? Or some combination of the above?

Arthur Max describes the evolution: "We started looking at bull rings because the bull ring is the archetype of the ancient Roman arena. But most of those we found were not usable because they were too small. They didn't have the scale that the actual Colosseum had. So we came to

87

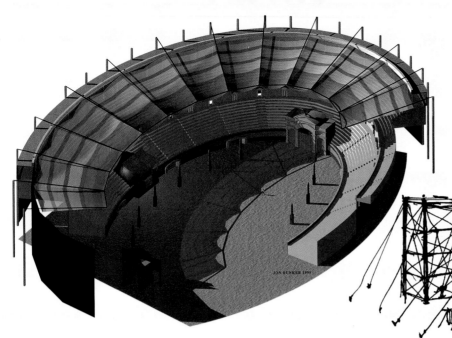

"AWNINGS WILL BE USED"

An ancient advertisement for games in Pompeii promised combat between gladiators, a "wild animal hunt," and the added amenity of an awning to shield spectators from the Mediterranean sun. Like other amphitheaters, the Colosseum featured such a sunshade, called a velarium—and like everything else about the building, it would have been huge. Roman literature contains many references to the velarium, and the Colosseum itself still bears evidence of its use, in the row of corbels encircling the upper story. Each supported a tall mast, which rose through a hole in the topmost cornice for stability, and to which the awning was rigged. No one knows exactly how the velarium was constructed or rigged, but most scholars believe that it was operated by sailors recruited from the nearby port of Ostia, who worked from atop the cornice.

Recreating the velarium and the lighting pattern it created over the stadium was a key issue for the filmmakers. With Gérôme's painting, *Pollice Verso*, in mind, Ridley Scott called for a brooding interplay of light and shade that spilled over both the live and CG-created parts of the arena and audience. "Everyone agreed that a practical velarium would be the best solution for giving the appropriate shadows on the partial Colosseum set," says VFX supervisor John Nelson. So a real sunshade was constructed, with a CG version produced later to complete the final film views of the full arena. As directed by Scott or cinematographer John Mathieson, the apparatus could be extended and retracted on a system of cables and pulleys, controlled by first assistant director Terry Needham and his team.

Mathieson says, "The sail makers and structural engineers who built the Millennium Dome in London came up with this design, which was made out of steel and tough PVC. There were something like 17 sails that we could pull out to have trapezoid shapes that went over the seating. These threw shadows down with stripes of light between where the sails didn't meet. At certain times of the day, ribbons of light would turn into beams of dust as the horses ran around, so it would be like a cathedral at times. I think it made a big difference in the way the battles look—like putting a big spotlight on the gladiators. Everybody else is in shadow and they're watching what's happening in the sun. It made it look more like theater rather than sport."

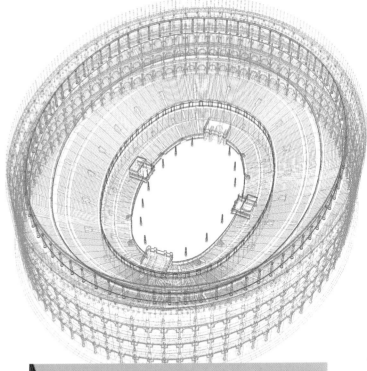

the conclusion that we would have to build a section of the arena, full size, and then extend the scale of the set using computer graphics and set extensions.

"From there, it was a matter of making models, using building blocks and developing a design. And once we had that, blowing it up to scale on paper. The process after that was to program our scaled drawings into a computer and generate three-dimensional visualizations from those designs—putting lens angles into the computer and seeing how much set we really had to have, the minimum amount that we could get away with. And finally, taking our architectural plans and building the set."

Max's construction team built a fragment of the Colosseum's first tier measuring approximately one-third the circumference of the original and 52 feet high. "It's only a fraction of the original but fairly accurate, we think, in detail," he notes. They also fabricated the bowels of the Colosseum, including a technologically crude but elaborate system of elevators to lift the gladiators onto the field of combat, and the entrance to the arena itself. The remainder of the Colosseum was achieved using state-of-the-art computer imaging (CGI), handled by visual effects supervisor John Nelson and Mill Film Ltd. in London. (See page 116.) Populating the Colosseum were 2,000 extras, who are seen cheering alongside 33,000 computer-generated spectators.

TOP: Computer-generated drawing of the Colosseum from above. Blue lines indicate portions of the set that were actually built (including the valerium); the remainder was created with CG effects. RIGHT: "Before and after" digital photos showing a tight view down the main street of the Rome set—in the upper photo, the existing buildings and partially built Colosseum, and below, the finished shot after CGI was added. Photos Mill Film Ltd.

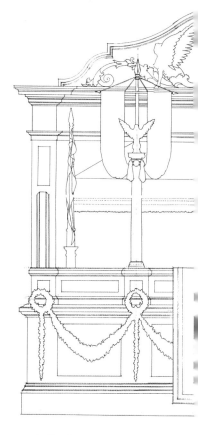

ABOVE LEFT: Inside a Roman tent in Germania. ABOVE: A senator's box in the Colosseum, drawn by Cliff Robinson. ABOVE RIGHT: Inside the emperor's palace.

DECORATING THE SETS

Gladiator's big action sequences are balanced by more intimate interior scenes that take place inside the Roman tents in Germania, at Proximo's training schools in both Africa and Rome, and within the emperor's palace in Rome.

The production design team worked to ensure that the director's vision was carried through consistently in the set design, decoration, and props. Every detail of the gladiators' world was gritty, harsh, and unforgiving; while the atmosphere inside Marcus Aurelius's campaign tents is sternly military with touches of warmth and luxury. And the interiors of imperial Rome are outscaled, baroque, and incredibly lavish—like the heightened vision of the Roman Empire Ridley Scott adopted from the painters he and Arthur Max studied.

These sets were all created and the shooting done on location, with natural lighting wherever possible. Thus they looked fully integrated with the outdoor scenes shot in the same place—

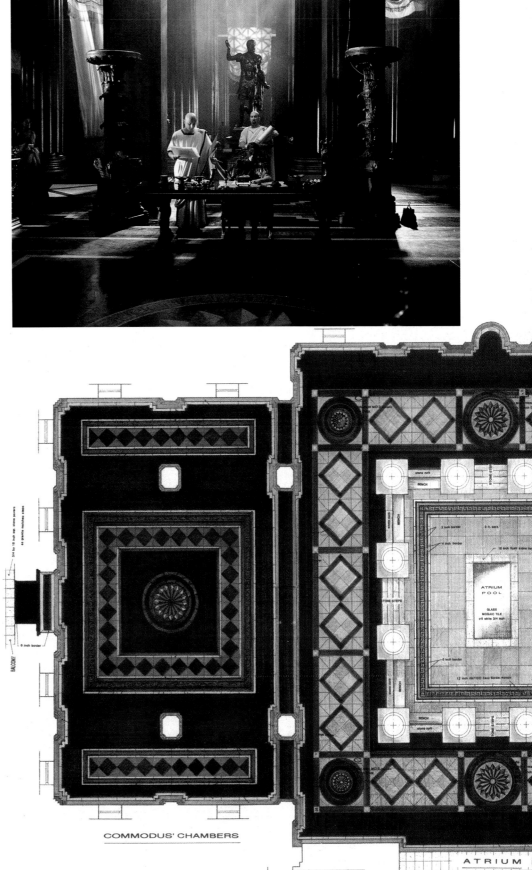

BELOW: *The Death of Caesar* by Jean-Léon Gérôme, 1859—one of several paintings that helped inform *Gladiator's* interior sets. Courtesy the Walters Art Gallery, Baltimore. BELOW RIGHT: Interior palace floor, layout by Arthur Max.

COMMODUS' CHAMBERS

ATRIUM

Ridley Scott deliberately avoided the look of a "studio" shoot. For example, Proximo's gladiator school was built into one of the ruined fortress buildings on Malta; the crew renovated collapsed ceilings and removed window and doorframes, so from certain angles the camera looks straight out to other parts of the set. For another touch of realism the Roman tents were pitched outdoors in England's Bourne Woods, so that you can see the tent walls quiver and candles flicker in the gusts of real winter wind.

The sumptuous, slightly menacing interiors of Commodus's palace in Rome were based chiefly on paintings by Lawrence Alma-Tadema. Arthur Max notes that the late 19th-century English artist was himself so obsessed with recreating ancient Rome that he had his own props made to stage scenes: bronze lamps, chairs carved from marble. Many details in the palace set—columns, floor mosaics, tall sculptural braziers—were borrowed from his paintings. But the filmmakers wanted to convey a sense of brooding darkness around Commodus, so they shifted from Alma-Tadema's pastel palette to more somber black and gold, dark reds and greens. Like real Roman houses, the palace set featured an atrium to admit natural light, which Scott relied on almost entirely to illuminate the scenes there.

The elaborate mosaic floor of Commodus's chambers was produced in linoleum by a renowned English fabricator to Max's design specifications and in custom, nonstandard col-

ABOVE: Main staircase in the residence of Senator Gracchus (Derek Jacobi, center). This set was created in one of the fortress buildings on Malta, by opening bricked-up rooms and adding set decor. Scenic artist Brian Bishop created fully executed frescoes for Gracchus's sitting room (not shown) and other sets. BELOW LEFT: Commodus's bed, drawn by John King. BELOW RIGHT: Study for a wall fresco in Proximo's apartment, by Benjamin Fernandez.

ors. The tiles were shipped to Malta in 140 boxes, accompanied by floor layers who spent weeks piecing the puzzle together. Commodus's magnificent carved and gilded throne was adapted by set decorator Crispian Sallis from a portrait of Napolean's coronation by one of the early 19th-century French classicists—again, because it was more dramatic than the actual Roman version. "We did lots of cutting and pasting from different sources," says Max, "and interpreted them as we felt was appropriate to our story."

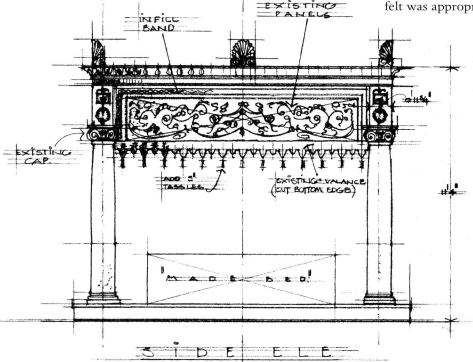

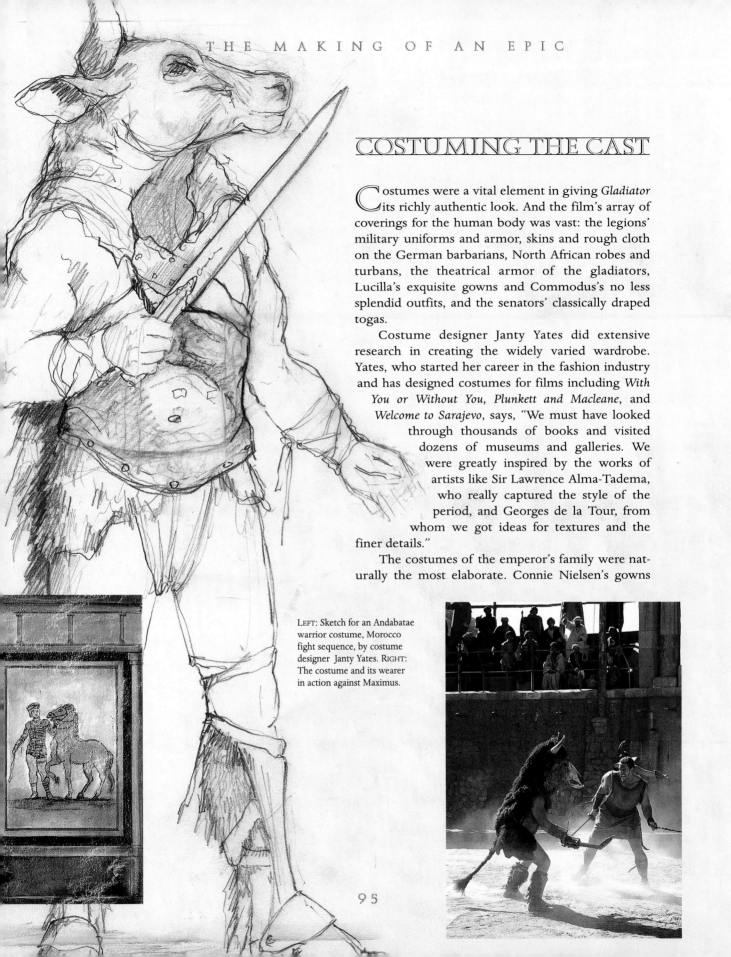

COSTUMING THE CAST

Costumes were a vital element in giving *Gladiator* its richly authentic look. And the film's array of coverings for the human body was vast: the legions' military uniforms and armor, skins and rough cloth on the German barbarians, North African robes and turbans, the theatrical armor of the gladiators, Lucilla's exquisite gowns and Commodus's no less splendid outfits, and the senators' classically draped togas.

Costume designer Janty Yates did extensive research in creating the widely varied wardrobe. Yates, who started her career in the fashion industry and has designed costumes for films including *With You or Without You, Plunkett and Macleane*, and *Welcome to Sarajevo*, says, "We must have looked through thousands of books and visited dozens of museums and galleries. We were greatly inspired by the works of artists like Sir Lawrence Alma-Tadema, who really captured the style of the period, and Georges de la Tour, from whom we got ideas for textures and the finer details."

The costumes of the emperor's family were naturally the most elaborate. Connie Nielsen's gowns

LEFT: Sketch for an Andabatae warrior costume, Morocco fight sequence, by costume designer Janty Yates. RIGHT: The costume and its wearer in action against Maximus.

95

Wolf Cape

Max: Felix
General

Old
Brass
Cuirass

Metal
Greaves
+
Arm Armour

Plain
Back
Plate

Wolf piece

OPPOSITE: Sketch for Lucilla's cape with fabric detail; the garment was cashmere, lined with silk. ABOVE: Janty Yates's drawing of Maximus' costume as general of the Felix Legions, showing fabric detail. LEFT: Maximus and Lucilla wearing their luxurious "wolfskin-trimmed" winter capes in Germania (faux fur was actually used). FAR RIGHT: Sketch for a Roman gentlewoman's dress.

were multilayered in luxurious fabrics like silk, satin, organza, and chiffon. The line of her dresses was achieved by wrapping a simple shift in bindings of contrasting color and texture. Over each dress Nielsen wore a stole draped around her arms, while another length of rich fabric formed a hooded cape. Gold thread was woven into the fabrics to give them a shimmer, and almost every garment was also embroidered by hand with gold thread, as well as semiprecious jewels.

All of the footwear was handmade in Rome, including the decorative sandals of Commodus and Lucilla, which were also hand-embroidered. The intricate designs of the royal jewelry were faithful to the fashion of the time. They were all handcrafted by England's noted jeweler Martin Adams, with the exception of one piece that Nielsen herself contributed. "In an antique store, I found a 2,000-year-old signet ring," she relates. "Wearing it made me feel more connected to the part."

The wardrobe had a similar effect on Joaquin Phoenix, who comments, "The minute I put on the costumes, I felt like I was in a completely different world. After a while, they didn't seem like costumes."

Like Nielsen, Phoenix was clothed in tunics and cloaks of silk, though his armor was decidedly less comfortable. "His armor had to be malleable to allow for movement, so it was made of rubber and then covered in leather," Yates reveals. "You can imagine how he felt in the hot sun of Malta." Yates created Commodus's stunning white armor ensemble to look like marble, based on Ridley Scott's idea that Commodus was trying to echo the statuary of his predecessors.

The physical demands of Russell Crowe's role required that his armor be much lighter, so all the pieces were made of foam and covered in leather. Moreover, every piece—including breastplates, hel-

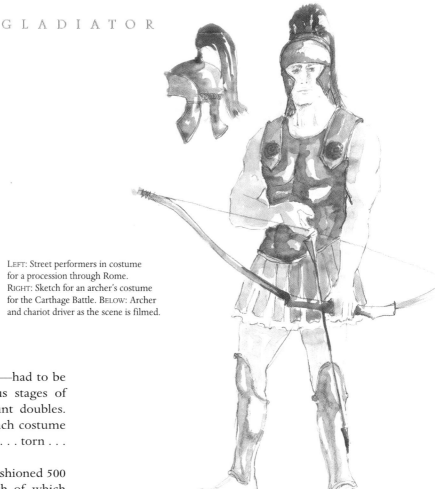

LEFT: Street performers in costume for a procession through Rome. RIGHT: Sketch for an archer's costume for the Carthage Battle. BELOW: Archer and chariot driver as the scene is filmed.

mets, arm and leg armor, and more—had to be duplicated 12 times over in various stages of wear, for Crowe as well as his stunt doubles. "There were different versions of each costume as scenes progressed: clean . . . dirty . . . torn . . . bloody," Yates says.

The costume department also fashioned 500 gladiator tunics in rough linen, each of which had to be distressed. In all, Yates, along with costume supervisor Rosemary "Frocks" Burrows, assistant designer Samantha Howarth, and their crew, had to create more than 10,000 costumes for the speaking cast and the thousands of extras.

Burrows also was responsible for setting up wardrobe facilities—what Yates called "costume villages"—which were used for warehousing, and for organizing space for the up to 2,000 extras per day to dress and have their hair and makeup done. In England, this included mud baths for the soldiers to provide the proper amount of battle grit. Burrows also found a Yorkshire farrier who could make the real chain mail Ridley Scott wanted.

ABOVE: Costume designer Janty Yates helps a Praetorian Guard with final costume adjustments. RIGHT: Costume sketch for an officer in the Felix Legions. BELOW: Sketch of Marcus Aurelius's costume, with inset photos of the finished costume and actor Richard Harris wearing it.

Marcus Aurelius Battle Armour

Rich Purple + Aged Bronze

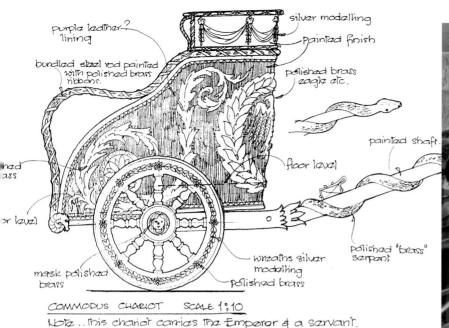

purple leather? lining

silver modelling

painted finish

bundled steel rod painted with polished brass ribbons

polished brass eagle etc.

painted shaft.

floor level

polished "brass" serpent

mask polished brass

wreaths silver modelling

polished brass

COMMODUS CHARIOT   SCALE 1:10

Note... this chariot carries the Emperor & a servant.

VEHICLES

ABOVE LEFT AND ABOVE: Preliminary production drawing of Commodus's chariot and a production photo showing the chariot as built, with a few details changed. All vehicles drawings on these pages by Cliff Robinson.

The characters in *Gladiator* travel the length and breadth of the Roman Empire—sometimes on horseback but most often in wheeled vehicles of various kinds. The Romans got very good at building roads—their only means of keeping the far-flung empire linked—and used a wide range of vehicles to transport armies and their goods, cart slaves and cargo, and carry the powerful in style.

The *Gladiator* production team designed and built vehicles for all these purposes and more, under the direction of Clifford Robinson, one of England's most experienced art directors for film vehicles. He and Arthur Max had once worked together on *Greystoke*, and at Max's behest, Robinson researched and drafted drawings that depict the needed vehicles in astonishing detail. His teams of carpenters, painters, and finishers built them all down to the last bolt on location in England, Morocco, and Malta.

Early in the film we see the massive, fully enclosed travel wagon in which Commodus and his sister Lucilla journey from Rome to the German front. Invented to convey a warlike image rather than historically based, it was made of hardwoods with a traditional steering mechanism and steel-rimmed wheels, and drawn by huge Shire draft horses. Other staff and baggage wagons made up Commodus's convoy; a Conestoga-style model was based on the only known example of Roman four-wheelers. In contrast, the wagon used to transport Maximus and the other gladiator-slaves to the provincial arena in Africa was an open affair made of wood and leather lashings, with a rod lengthwise down the center to which the slaves were manacled.

But Robinson's pièce de résistance was the film's chariots. These not only

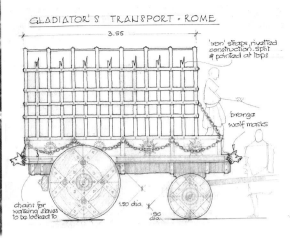

GLADIATOR'S TRANSPORT · ROME

3.55

'iron' straps, rivetted
construction, split
& pointed at tops

bronze
wolf masks

chains for
walking slaves
to be locked to

1.50 dia.

.90
dia.

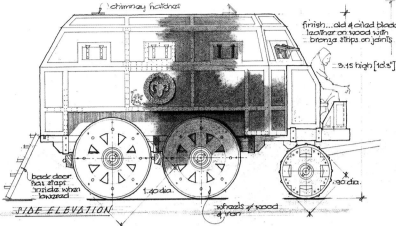

'chimney hatches

finish...old & oiled black
leather on wood with
bronze strips on joints

3.15 high [10'3"]

back door
has steps
inside when
lowered

1.40 dia.

.90 dia.

wheels of wood
& iron

SIDE ELEVATION

had to look realistic and opulent, but they had to work solidly and reliably during the spectacular Carthage Battle, in which chariot teams carrying archers hurtle around the arena in combat with Proximo's gladiators. The chariot in which Commodus makes his entrance into Rome featured purple leather lining, polished brass wheels and trim, and modeled reliefs of the imperial laurel and eagles. In a later scene, the gladiator Tigris of Gaul enters the arena in a chariot adorned with a roaring tiger.

For the chariots, the filmmakers found plenty of historical reference in Roman triumphal statuary, mosaics, and bas-reliefs like Trajan's Column. In all, 24 chariots were built, of which 16 were used in the battle scene—though only six actually appear on screen. Some were specially constructed for stunt work, others customized to accommodate camera mounts for combat-level angles. Robinson also designed and built trollies to transport animal cages, various human-drawn devices for hauling bodies out of the arena or raking up the blood, as well as the war machines used in the Germania battle.

ABOVE LEFT: Proximo's gladiator transport.
ABOVE: Commodus's wagon featured modeled bronze doors, wheels of wood and iron, and steps that lowered from the back for easy entry. Inside it was decorated with frescoes and covered in leather, with elaborate metalwork accessories.
BELOW: Commodus's wagon in the background of the Germania encampment set.

FAR LEFT: Chariot detail. LEFT: Cliff Robinson's color-coded chart itemizing all the needed vehicles. BELOW: Commodus's Germania travel convoy and the North African slave convoy (left).

LEFT: Concept study of
a gladiator in boar-tusk
helmet, by Sylvain Despretz.
BELOW: A gladiator in full rig.

WEAPONS AND ARMOR

More than 2,500 weapons were designed and manufactured for *Gladiator* by supervising armorer Simon Atherton and his team. At the height of the Germania battle, the cast, stuntmen, and thousands of extras fight hand to hand with broadswords, axes, spears, and daggers; earlier in the battle, some 16,000 flaming arrows were sent aloft by the Roman archers. Later in the film, the gladiators ply their trade using everything from the standard short sword (the *gladius*) to spears (*pilum*) to maces, tridents, ball-and-chain, and bronze clubs.

Many of the armaments were original concepts, resulting from a combination of research and innovation. Atherton explains, "There was not much reference to be found in books for weaponry and armor from this period. So, taking ideas from what we know about subsequent periods and trying to imagine the evolution of certain weapons—with the understanding that they did mostly close-quarter fighting—we were able to come up with some designs that would have been feasible at that time."

Atherton especially welcomed Ridley Scott's challenge to come up with the Roman equivalent of an automatic weapon: the multi-firing crossbow used by the female gladiators. But he is also proud of the conventional archery showcased in the film. "Special effects had machines that could launch batteries of arrows into the air at once. But our guys firing in the usual way could get them into the air pretty quickly, too." Some of the weapons were special props made of rubber, leather, or other soft materials "so people can get hit in the face and really clobbered," notes Atherton—but such substitutes lack the authentic heft and glint of metal, so the real thing was used wherever possible.

102

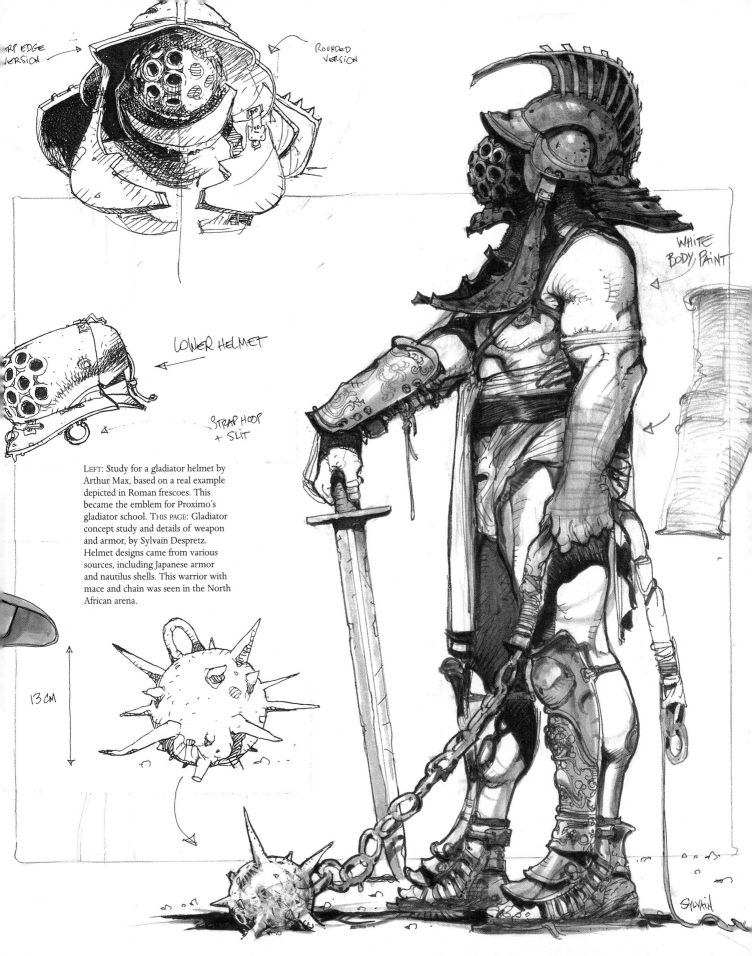

SHARP EDGE VERSION

ROUNDED VERSION

LOWER HELMET

STRAP HOOP + SLIT

13 CM

WHITE BODY PAINT

LEFT: Study for a gladiator helmet by Arthur Max, based on a real example depicted in Roman frescoes. This became the emblem for Proximo's gladiator school. THIS PAGE: Gladiator concept study and details of weapon and armor, by Sylvain Despretz. Helmet designs came from various sources, including Japanese armor and nautilus shells. This warrior with mace and chain was seen in the North African arena.

SYLVAIN

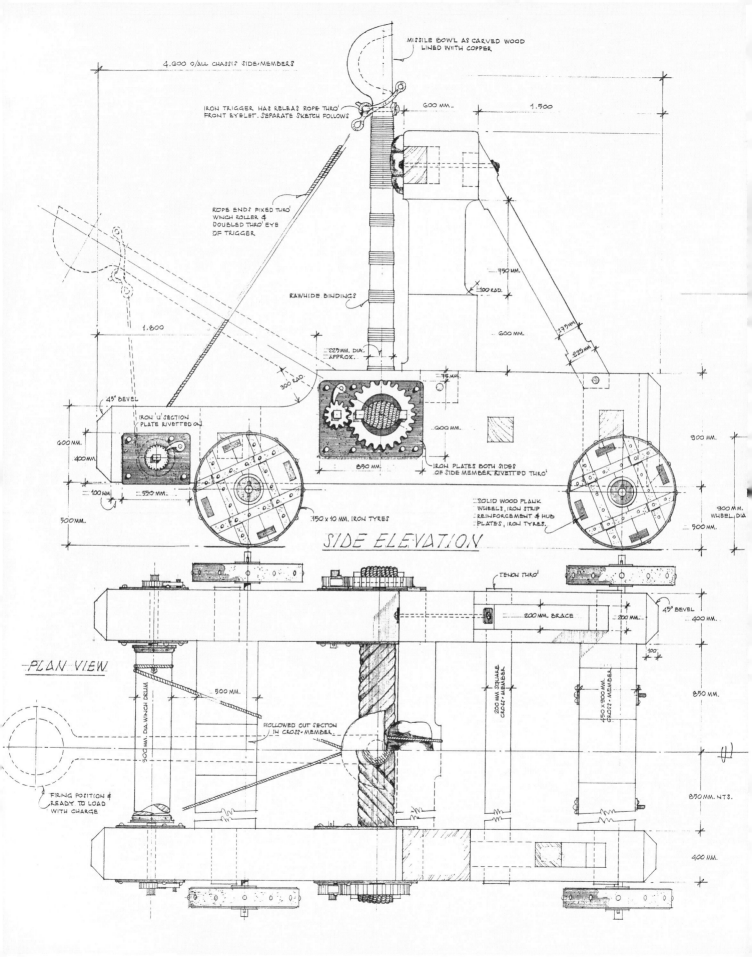

4.600 O/ALL CHASSIS SIDE·MEMBERS

MISSILE BOWL AS CARVED WOOD
LINED WITH COPPER

600 MM.

1.500

IRON TRIGGER HAS RELEAS ROPE THRO'
FRONT EYELET. SEPARATE SKETCH FOLLOWS

ROPE ENDS FIXED THRO'
WINCH ROLLER &
DOUBLED THRO' EYE
OF TRIGGER

750 MM.

100 RAD.

RAWHIDE BINDINGS

1.800

600 MM.

175 MM.

225 MM.

225 MM. DIA.
APPROX.

300 RAD.

75 MM.

43° BEVEL

IRON 'U' SECTION
PLATE RIVETTED ON

600 MM.

900 MM.

400 MM

600 MM.

850 MM.

IRON PLATES BOTH SIDES
OF SIDE MEMBER RIVETTED THRO'

900 MM.
WHEEL DIA.

100 MM.

550 MM.

750 x 10 MM. IRON TYRES

SOLID WOOD PLANK
WHEELS, IRON STRIP
REINFORCEMENT & HUB
PLATES, IRON TYRES.

500 MM.

500MM.

SIDE ELEVATION

TENON THRO'

45° BEVEL

400 MM.

PLAN VIEW

200 MM. BRACE

200 MM.

100

500 MM.

300 MM. DIA. WINCH DRUM

HOLLOWED OUT SECTION
IN CROSS·MEMBER

200 MM SQUARE
CROSS·MEMBERS

450 x 900 MM.
CROSS·MEMBER

850 MM.

850 MM. NTS.

FIRING POSITION &
READY TO LOAD
WITH CHARGE

400 MM.

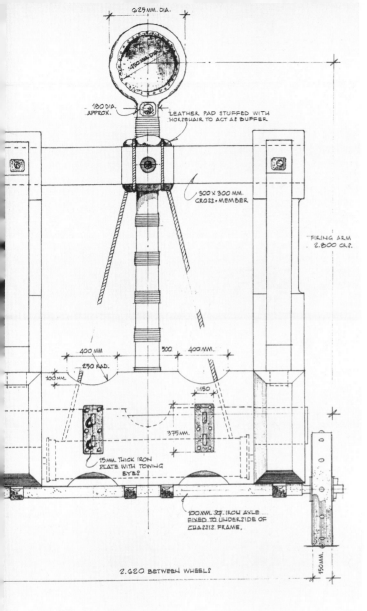

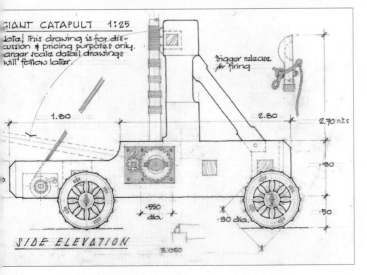

Atherton also served as a consultant to the costume department in the design and function of the helmets and some armor. Again, some of the designs were authentically Roman, like the flaring helmet seen on the preceding page, while others, like the elaborate Tiger mask and bodygear, were invented for the story.

The larger war machines used by the Roman army—fully functional catapults and the deadly "scorpion," which fired volleys of arrows—were the province of vehicle designer Cliff Robinson. Two full-size catapults were built, each weighing about a ton, and could generate awesome power,

which called for careful rehearsal. Ridley Scott says, "We believe the Romans could hurl missiles 250 meters with these machines. Ours went about 150 yards, which is still a good sling. You wind them down with a thick, twisted hawser that goes around a giant winch, then knock a pin out, and the arm flies up with such force that the whole massive machine will leap off the ground."

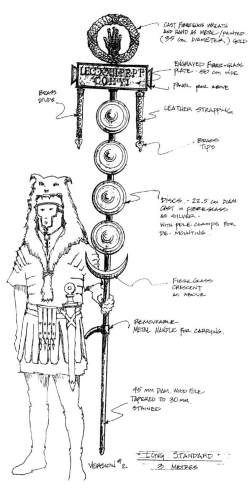

CAST FIBREGLASS WREATH
AND HAND AS METAL/PAINTED
(35 CM DIAMETER.) GOLD

ENGRAVED FIBREGLASS
PLATE · 50 CM WIDE

PANEL FOR ABOVE

BRASS
STUDS

LEATHER STRAPPING

BRASS
TIPS

DISCS · 22.5 CM DIAM
CAST IN FIBREGLASS
AS SILVER.
WITH POLE CLAMPS FOR
DE-MOUNTING.

FIBREGLASS
CRESCENT
AS ABOVE

REMOVEABLE
METAL HANDLE FOR CARRYING.

45 MM DIAM. WOOD POLE
TAPERED TO 30 MM.
STAINED

VERSION #2   LONG STANDARD
3 METRES

ABOVE AND BELOW: Drawings by Arthur Max of the Roman legions' battlefield gear. RIGHT: A legionnaire holds a standard similar to that in the drawing, but topped with the Felix Legion's name and emblem.

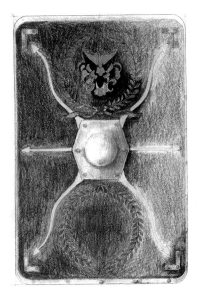

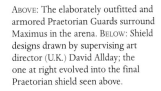

ABOVE: The elaborately outfitted and
armored Praetorian Guards surround
Maximus in the arena. BELOW: Shield
designs drawn by supervising art
director (U.K.) David Allday; the
one at right evolved into the final
Praetorian shield seen above.

SWORDPLAY AND STUNTS

Like their characters, Russell Crowe, Djimon Hounsou, and Ralf Moeller—the former bodybuilding champ who plays the formidable Hakan—shared the tremendous physical demands of being gladiators. Together with a group of highly skilled stuntmen, led by stunt coordinator Phil Neilson, the actors executed fight scenes that would have rivaled the training at Proximo's gladiator school.

"I've done some pretty physical stuff before, but this was unrelenting," Crowe attests. "At some point in the middle, I started thinking, 'Maybe I should have taken the role where I was a bus conductor.'" Ridley Scott concurs. "After a big fight scene I would try to give Russell a few days in a row of just walking and talking, so to speak, but it didn't always work out that way. There were some days with battle scenes end on

end, so he was aching in every muscle and bone."

That being the case, Crowe got a big laugh from a directive he received during filming. "They sent me a memo asking me not to play soccer because I might get hurt. At that point I'd been doing one massive fight scene after another, so I sent back a memo saying, 'I can wrestle with four tigers but I can't play a game of soccer? Get over it. Love, Russell.'"

In contrast to modern war epics, the battle sequences in *Gladiator* involved close sword fighting, requiring intricate staging and long rehearsals to ensure everyone's safety. Fight master Nicholas Powell, whose previous credits include *Braveheart*, was responsible with Neilson for choreographing the film's myriad sword fights. "The individual fights in this film were an opportunity to do something different," says

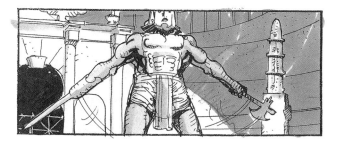

RIGHT: Concept drawing of the Tigris of Gaul helmet adapted in part from a French fire brigade helmet, by Sylvain Despretz.

LEFT: Storyboards by Sylvain Despretz of the fight between Maximus and Tigris of Gaul ("Tiger"), which involved some of the trickiest swordplay in the film. ABOVE AND RIGHT: Tiger and Maximus in the arena. Tiger's use of a battle axe as well as a sword arose from early discussions of the scene and how Maximus would finally defeat him. OVERLEAF: One of the difficult horse stunts in the Carthage Battle scene.

Powell, "because obviously no one knows exactly how they fought in this period.

"So you do your research . . . find out what kind of swords they used and how those weapons feel when they move through the air, how it would cut a person, and so on. And then adapt what you've learned to the story and what looks right for the camera. I try to impose a set of rules for each kind of fighting and to make the fights very fluid, so that one move flows naturally into the next." Powell also had to train all the actors and stuntmen, as well as the 1,000 extras who took part in the opening battle. His first priority was Russell Crowe, so weeks ahead of principal photography, Powell went to Australia to work one-on-one with the actor.

Ridley Scott notes, "All the actors had a lot to learn in terms of this kind of fighting. There was a tremendous amount of swordplay, which com-

pelled everyone to remember exact movement and placement to avoid getting something broken . . . or their head taken off," he adds, only half kidding.

Powell explains, "Ridley wanted close fighting, which looks better on screen but has slightly more intrinsic risk, especially since we were using primarily metal weapons. It's really a matter of getting the choreography down perfectly and keeping the guys on the ball all the time. They could never think, 'Well, we've done it ten times, so we're okay.' All you need is someone in the wrong place, someone to hit your arm, and your hand moves. . . . They had to concentrate every single time."

Djimon Hounsou, as Juba, can attest to that. During one scene, "I was fighting the guy with the horned bull-head mask. At one point the guy got up and turned his head suddenly, and the

horn missed my eye by an inch or two and left a deep cut in my shoulder."

Many of the gorier stunts involved collaboration between live-action shooting, special-effects prosthetics work, and visual effects done with bluescreen and computers. In the Carthage Battle, for example, one of the female archers is graphically sliced in two by the sharp blade attached to a chariot axle, and the Germania battle also called for some severed limbs.

Some of the most exciting stunt work came in the Carthage Battle, as chariots careen around Proximo's gladiators in the Colosseum. This turned out to be one of Ridley Scott's chief causes for anxiety, because the space available to build the stadium was about 15 percent smaller than was ideal. "The chariot weighs about 500 pounds, and those horses can move like lightning," Scott explains. "They're coming up that ramp and into

the arena at full gallop, and they have to keep at full speed while they're in the shot—otherwise it looks terrible. But once they've passed an imaginary line, they have to stop. They can't turn, because they're going too fast; they just have to rein in and slow down fast. And I knew I was 15 percent short, so it was really tricky. They were grazing the other end of the stadium."

Scott has high praise for his stunt team, including stunt coordinator Neilson and all the stuntmen (and women). "We built up a great team of stunt men—half of them were gladiators, really. They would start out being German troops or Roman troops, then we'd use them again, redressed and reconformed, in North Africa. And then (if we're not starting to recognize them too much) again in Rome. A good stunt man is invaluable because he sees that accidents don't happen—and also that it looks good."

projects, including *Amistad*. In Morocco the animal roster included tigers, leopards, and giraffes (two of each), four lions, ostriches and vultures (ten each). Shooting in Malta called for five tigers, four lions, two zebras, four dogs, two oxen, and an elephant. (Not all these animals appear in the final cut.) Reynolds's associate trainer was Thierry Le Portier. Horse master on the film was the veteran Steve Dent, assisted by Peter White.

Finding the exotic animals they needed in Morocco was a particular challenge. As Lustig points out, transporting wild animals between countries is strictly regulated today, and most European countries would not ship animals to North Africa. "But when I was in Rabat, I saw that they have an excellent zoo. And they did give us permission to use some of their animals. Of course, these are not animals that have been raised and trained for this work—they are really wild. But everyone survived and we sent all the animals back healthy."

ANIMAL KINGDOM

The production executive responsible for the crucial work involving animals in *Gladiator* was Branko Lustig, whose experience with animal wrangling for movies goes back to his early career in the 1950s, in his native Yugoslavia. During World War II the army had still used horses, and after the war Lustig's company, Yadrim Film, bought up many of them. "So whenever the Italian filmmakers wanted to shoot a historical picture that called for horses, they came to us," the producer recalls.

It was Lustig who brought in chief animal trainer Paul "Sled" Reynolds, who also sourced most of the animals that appear in the film. Reynolds had worked on other DreamWorks

TIGER, TIGER

"Ridley told us that he wanted the tiger fight to be very violent and very scary," says chief animal trainer Sled Reynolds. But how to accomplish that without endangering the actors and crew? The answer is, with the utmost patience and the help of a top digital effects team and editor.

Scott had storyboarded the whole sequence and knew what he wanted, down to the last shot. With the cameras rolling, the animal handlers would use bait and other enticements to coax the tigers to lunge, leap, and roar, while controlling each with a chain that ran through a ring affixed to the arena floor. Each move on a tiger's part was matched with a reaction from Russell Crowe (or his stunt double), usually shot at a different time against the same background. Film editor Pietro Scalia would view daily rushes and see how much of the desired shot was achieved, then ask for reshoots on what was still missing.

The process depended greatly on the animals' cooperation—which often wasn't forthcoming. "We had allowed four days to shoot the tigers," Ridley Scott recalls, "and it took weeks." VFX supervisor John Nelson concurs, "I had a whole camera crew working three feet away from a 600-pound wild animal. That really gets your adrenaline going."

Scott made sure that his star wasn't allowed closer than 15 feet or so of the tigers during shooting, although Crowe did many of his other stunts for real. This probably wasn't over-cautious: one of the handlers had a narrow escape one day when a tiger doubled back on her chain and knocked him to the ground briefly, but no damage was done. "Unfortunately, they're so quick that if they do decide to grab you, you hardly ever see it coming," says Reynolds.

ABOVE: Chief animal trainer Sled Reynolds works with one of the tigers. Of the four tigers used, the two more docile ones were from the U.S.; the other two were from France and, not being hand-raised, were less predictable. BELOW: Storyboards of the Tiger Fight sequence by Sylvain Despretz.

ABOVE: A camera operator harnessed to an ATV-drawn trailer rig captures a ground-level shot of the onrushing chariots. BELOW: Drawing of the ramp system used for the tigers' entrance into the arena, by Sylvain Despretz.

PRACTICAL "ELEVATOR" COLOSSEUM
TIGER RAMP TRICK

The filmmakers chose to spare viewers a fully realistic view of how the Romans used animals in their blood sports. In the days of Empire, hunters ranged throughout the Mediterranean world capturing wild animals and transporting them to Italy to slake the Romans' insatiable interest in seeing—and then slaughtering—exotic creatures. So relentlessly were animals like the big cats hunted that they soon grew rare throughout the Near East, where they had once been abundant. Records indicate that one emperor killed as many as 5,000 animals in a three-day stretch of games. As well as "hunting" animals in the arena, or using them to maul and kill human victims, a popular event was the pitting of different species against each other—animals that were never natural enemies, such as a gorilla and a bear. Still, the experienced

Reynolds marvels at the logistics the Romans conquered to get their animals: "Can you imagine hauling elephants and bulls and rhinos on those old ships? It had to be horrendous—especially for the animals."

In the Germania sequence, Reynolds's main task was working with the trained German Shepherd who stood in for the wolf of Rome—General Maximus's companion in the battle. "We were meant to use real wolves, but we couldn't get them into England because of rabies quarantine"—typical of the challenges involved in importing animals.

Reynolds's biggest challenge on the film was working with the tigers that spring into the arena to attack Maximus during his rigged fight with the gladiator Tigris of Gaul. Branko Lustig knew what they were up against in getting this scene to work: "Tigers are just big cats; you can tell them what to do, but they don't always listen."

"I tell people that working with animals is a lot like driving very fast. As long as you concentrate and are real careful, you shouldn't have a problem, but you can always end up off the road. It's the same with tigers and lions. The only predictability is the unpredictability."

—ANIMAL TRAINER SLED REYNOLDS

VISUAL AND SPECIAL EFFECTS

Russell Crowe very accurately calls *Gladiator* "a magnificent marriage of old-fashioned filmmaking values and absolute cutting-edge technology." It is a given that the movie could not have looked the way it does without the magic of special and visual effects, which helped the filmmakers generate maximum impact in the great opening battle, in the heart-stopping gladiator action scenes, and in Ridley Scott's expansive vision of ancient Rome.

The complementary roles of visual effects (optical and digital effects realized with computers) and special effects (mechanical, prosthetic, and pyrotechnic work) were closely planned in pre-production. Task one was to assemble the best personnel for the project, and Scott named as his chief deputies visual effects supervisor John Nelson and special effects supervisor Neil Courbold. Nelson's recent credits include the romantic drama *City of Angels*, as well as the thriller *Anaconda*, *The Cable Guy*, *Wolf*, and *The Pelican Brief*. Corbould, who comes from a family of special effects craftsmen, has won BAFTA awards for his work on *Saving Private Ryan* and *The Fifth Element*.

The crucial job of compositing VFX shots was awarded to Mill Film in London, a digital post-production facility founded in 1990 and whose shareholders include Ridley Scott and his brother Tony. Mill's recent credits include *Enemy of the State* and *Babe: Pig in the City*. Other key players were director of photography John Mathieson and editor Pietro Scalia. Quickly the team got down to the business of budgeting the effects work—figuring out how much of the action would be live, what practical effects might be used, and how much digital work was needed.

Scott made his approach clear from the start: "Ridley was adamant that he didn't want effects for effects sake," Nelson says. "He wanted to use

effects in the story to broaden the scope of wide shots and show the overwhelming, oppressive size of Rome."

The concept for each shot began with the director's own pen-and-ink drawings, which his colleagues call "Ridleygrams." Artist Sylvain Despretz used these as his guide to storyboard each shot, and also helped Nelson prepare VFX breakdowns illustrating areas where CGI effects would enhance and extend practical action and locations.

Once the locations were decided, they could begin plotting out the details of set design to be accomplished with VFX. "Each location lent the film its own graphic quality," says Nelson. "Ridley talked about how the beginning of the movie would have an overall blue cast, with soft, cool northern light and just a little gold coming from the fires. Then, as we followed the arc of Max's character, the light became much harder, eventually taking us to Rome, which would be

ABOVE: "Before and after" digital photos of the Germania battlefield, as filmed with real extras and after CGI work multiplied the Roman legions and added in background fire and explosions. BELOW: A VFX plate depicting the vast expanse of Roman tents, another CG effect. OPPOSITE: Sylvain Despretz's drawing of the Roman battle line. LEFT: Visual effects supervisor John Nelson.

Digital photo showing part of the overhead "blimp shot" created by Mill Film, in which many of the elements—buildings, the Colosseum exterior, and pedestrians—were created with CGI.

completely golden with deep, crisp shadows."

Nelson traveled to England in October 1998 to work with Mill Film supervisors Tim Burke and Rob Harvey, CG supervisor Laurent Hugueniot, and VFX producer Nikki Penny. Together they developed concepts for building the Roman capital and populating its Colosseum—while also planning for the opening in Germania.

For the Germania battle, the major tasks were to show the might of the Roman army and how technologically advanced it was, to arrange pyrotechnic effects for the fiery climax, and to create realistic carnage through a combination of prosthetics and digital work. Conveying the vast scale of the Roman encampment and the battle was challenging, in part because the production had fewer extras than they'd hoped for. Scott and Nelson planned to multiply 500 costumed extras in a master shot that panned left to right from the hilltop point-of-view of Emperor Marcus Aurelius. "Tim Burke came up with the idea of shooting VistaVision (the standard for creating digital 'plates' of a shot), then tiling three locked-off shots together," says Nelson.

The VFX team also developed techniques to move the giant catapults in or out of a shot and to extend their firing range. Visual effects added hundreds of flaming arrows to those fired by the Roman archers, as well as smoke and explosions behind the Germanic army.

Practical special effects, meanwhile, were laying hundreds of yards of two-inch steel pipe under the forest floor, into which propane was pumped to stage the conflagration. Neil Corbould's crew spent six weeks rigging the pipes and implementing safety measures. "We paced the set with Ridley and he decided where he wanted the horses coming through," says Corbould. "We created six diagonal lines of fire, staggered at intervals, so that when the camera shot straight into the scene, the cavalry appeared to be engulfed by one giant wall of flame."

Later, after Maximus makes his heroic but futile effort to return home and save his family,

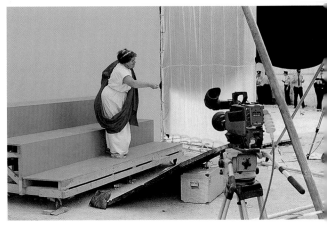

LEFT: Thanks to CGI work, the Colosseum facade rises to its full four stories in this digital image. ABOVE: The greenscreen photo booth set up at the Colosseum site to digitally capture extras in a variety of poses and costumes. This enabled Mill Film to fill the stands of the Colosseum with spectators. BELOW: The Colosseum interior before and after CGI.

he takes a blow to the head and is carted off to be sold as a slave. VFX editor Wesley Sewell captured Maximus's dreamlike sense of dislocation in a hallucinatory sequence that combined production footage of Crowe with backgrounds shot on location and stock footage treated digitally to influence color and frame speed.

The effects crews moved from location to location with the production. In Morocco, the emphasis shifted to prosthetic and mechanical effects, with extensive "amputation effects" needed for the fight scene in which the gladiators are chained together. Says Corbould, "We set up a workshop in a big tent, including a latex facility, so we if needed more prosthetic pieces we could just run them up the night before." Because most of the Morocco set was the existing town of Ouarzazate, and the arena was built physically, the VFX work was limited to adding in some circling vultures over the amphitheater.

Just as the story reaches its climax in Rome, so did the efforts of the effects team. The approach to realizing Scott's concept for the city grew out of much discussion. "We talked about

ABOVE: Live action filming of the scene in which Commodus enters Rome, and right, the scene completed with CGI. Ridley Scott wanted Commodus's grand entrance into Rome to echo Nazi-era propaganda films like Leni Reifenstahl's *Triumph of the Will*. "We saturated the scene in monochrome tones," notes Nelson, "added rose petals falling, multiplied the crowds, and extended the buildings so Rome stretches off into the distance." The broad plaza with its massed Praetorian Guards is an almost completely CG environment. BELOW: VFX plates generated by Mill Film with Ridley Scott's hand-drawn revisions. The atmospheric shot of birds flocking over Rome was important to the director, and done entirely with CGI.

using miniatures early on," says Nelson. But the final solution was to maximize the Malta ruins by building onto them physically and constructing a fragment of the Colosseum to actual size. The CG work focused on extending the sets as needed, adding crowds, and achieving the lighting effects the director wanted.

The heart and soul of Rome, in the second century and in the film, was the Colosseum. Nelson notes: "At the time of our story, the Colosseum was around 100 years old, so it had to appear to have aged accordingly. Ridley wanted a view of Rome that looked lived in and starting to crumble a bit. He worked with Arthur Max to create a patina for the Colosseum, and once this was established, the digital artists at Mill Film could lock into these textures." The highly complex effects work on the Colosseum included sun studies, radiosity analysis (an artificial light-simulation rendering technique), and photogrammetry—the digital projection of photorealistic textures onto computer-generated geometry.

The first glimpse of the Colosseum stands out even among all this CG artistry. This so-called "blimp shot," a Super Bowl-style aerial point of view, reveals and traverses the Colosseum, to arrive at a down-view of a combat in progress. Another remarkable shot later on is the 360-degree Steadicam shot that circles around Maximus and his gladiators as they enter the arena for the first time and take in the spectacle, including vast crowds that fill the stands.

For this and other shots, the VFX team needed "a robust strategy" for multiplying their 2,000 extras into some 70,000 screaming, gesticulating fans. "Laurence Hugueniot came up with the idea of shooting tiles of the crowd and placing them into our 3D portions of the stadium," relates Nelson. To make those tiles, the Mill team shot crowd performers against a greenscreen with bluescreen slashes of color in their costumes. These could then be digitally re-colored for variety. A greenscreen photo-booth was built on site, with three Betacam cameras capturing each extra in a range of poses: staring, cheering, nonchalantly talking, thumbs up, thumbs down. The shots were positioned by computer into seats in the Colosseum, using Mill Film's proprietary Crowd Builder software.

Down on the sandy arena floor, practical and visual effects teamed up with stunt work and editing to create breathtaking fights like the Carthage Battle, in which six chariots race to their destruction and their occupants meet gory ends, and the Tiger Fight, where very real tigers appear to come within a hairsbreadth of slashing Russell Crowe to ribbons. In the Carthage Battle, Phil Neilson's stunt team and Pietro Scalia's editorial wizardry were complemented by Neil Corbould's explosive physical effects, while digital effects were used primarily to complete wide shots.

Special effects supervisor Corbould and stunt coordinator Neilson had been plotting scenes of graphic mayhem since early in preproduction. One of the most dramatic prosthetic effects was the decapitation of a Germanic soldier against a tree, which goes by quickly in the final cut. Another is the scene in the Carthage Battle where a female charioteer (a fiberglass-and-silicone dummy) is severed in half by a blade projecting from the chariot wheel.

Staging and shooting the Tiger Fight called on everyone's ingenuity—plus the services of an animatronic tiger created under Corbould's supervision by Pauline Fowler at Animated Extras.

ABOVE: Ridley Scott indicates how the animatronic tiger will leap at Maximus. BELOW, LEFT AND CENTER: A lunging (real) tiger and a fallen Russell Crowe as Maximus, and RIGHT: the two elements fused into one shot through CGI.

The full-size, weighted and articulated tiger puppet could be positioned standing with its paws over Maximus's shoulders, as depicted in the storyboards. At another point the puppet tiger was suspended from wires for a leaping shot.

After the human performers had been filmed, Nelson's VFX unit shot the tigers, duplicating the same camera angles and lenses. "We shot the tiger striking at his handler as he baited her with a piece of meat," Nelson says. "We pulled the tiger from that plate, added her to our clean plate, and threw in a little foreground dust to help blend her into the scene." Close-up interaction was achieved with a combination of live tiger action, glimpses of Corbould's animatronics, and a subtle glint of computer-generated steel when Maximus stabs the tiger.

After principal photography wrapped, the Mill Film crew returned to their computers in London; Scott, Scalia, and Nelson went back to Los Angeles; and postproduction work began. As VFX plates emerged from London, the images were transmitted to Scott via Mill's high-speed broadband connection. The eight-hour time difference actually worked to the project's advantage, creating an around-the-clock production line. Scott made six trips to London during postproduction, often sitting and working at the compositing machine with an artist for hours. The final tally of VFX shots created for the film came to 90, with approximately 9 minutes of the film's final running time being generated by Mill Film.

John Nelson recalls, "After we screened our first assembly of this movie, Ridley told me that one of the things he was most proud of was that it didn't feel like a big VFX movie. That was a real compliment," he adds, "not only to all the visual effects artists who worked on the film but also to Pietro Scalia. All the elements come together in such a mix that you become enthralled and overwhelmed by the cinematic mood. The VFX were there to support the story and the characters, and those were really strong."

ABOVE: Russell Crowe, in the grip of the (animatronic) tiger, desperately strikes the foot of his opponent, Tigris—a prosthetic limb. BELOW: Special effects floor supervisor Paul Corbould adjusts the highly detailed prosthetic head of a Germanic warrior beheaded in battle.

"To Our Friend, Oliver Reed"

On May 2, 1999, with about three weeks of shooting remaining on *Gladiator*, actor Oliver Reed died in Malta of apparent heart failure; he was 61. "I got quite a shock when I heard it," says Richard Harris, who plays Marcus Aurelius. "It's a shame, because this movie would have revived his career." Adds Russell Crowe, "Oliver went out the way he lived his life. I think it's one of his best performances in the last ten years—so this can be a memorial to him."

That performance was all but complete—however, a few crucial scenes with Reed's character, Proximo, remained to be shot. The decision was made to use post-production sleight of hand and a minor script rewrite to make sure that Reed's last bravura turn would be seen. "It was like a jigsaw puzzle," says Ridley Scott. "We reorganized three shots of his close-ups from three different scenes." Then, he continues, "I had his body double walk up to the camera, stand, and talk, and then I put Oliver's CGI head on the body."

John Nelson adds, "When Oliver passed on, we were all pretty shaken. He had given such a great performance, but Ridley, Pietro, the producers and I knew we would have to use a few subtle VFX to finish his part of the movie. Pietro selected footage of Oliver from existing shots, and we put him into new backgrounds for the scenes he had left to do, in some cases changing the color of his costume." He concludes, "What we did was small compared to our other tasks on the film. What Oliver did was much greater. He gave an inspiring, moving performance. All we did was help him finish it."

ABOVE: The late Oliver Reed as Proximo in a production photo. RIGHT: Oliver Reed's CG-created image as seen in the last few scenes.

A DREAM THAT WAS ROME

THE STORY OF *GLADIATOR*

GERMANIA

The year is 180 A.D. Emperor Marcus Aurelius and his legions have been campaigning along the Danube for many weary years, holding back the Germanic tribes that threaten the Roman Empire's borders. The Felix Legions' brilliant commander is General Maximus Decimus Meridius—a native of Spain, loyal soldier of Rome, and trusted servant of the emperor—who has now been absent from his beloved home and family for "two years, two hundred sixty-four days, and this morning."

A great battle is about to be joined. The Germans. Maximus himself leads the climactic cavalry charge through the blazing forest to annihilate the enemy.

After the victory feast, the emperor, aged and gravely ill, summons Maximus to his tent and bestows on him a weighty and unwanted gift: to lead Rome as *princeps* after Marcus's death, and restore its republican heritage. (His daughter, Lucilla, has the talent to govern though as a woman cannot.) But when the emperor's long-estranged son, Commodus, learns of the plan, he murders his father, claims the imperial

Germans are massed in the forest across the valley from Marcus's encampment, and the Romans' emissary has come back dead, headless, strapped to his galloping horse. Far outnumbered, the legions nonetheless prevail in the terrible fight through their superior discipline and deadly machinery of war that rains fire upon the throne, and orders Maximus and his family murdered. As Commodus prepares to return in triumph to Rome, the doomed Maximus turns the tables on his Praetorian executioners, takes their horses, and rides hard across Europe back to his vineyard estate in the Spanish hills.

EDITOR'S NOTE: In this part of the book we convey the film's story in a brief synopsis of each of its three "acts," followed by action scenes in the vivid storyboard art of Sylvain Despretz, and excerpts from the final screenplay illustrated with production still photos.

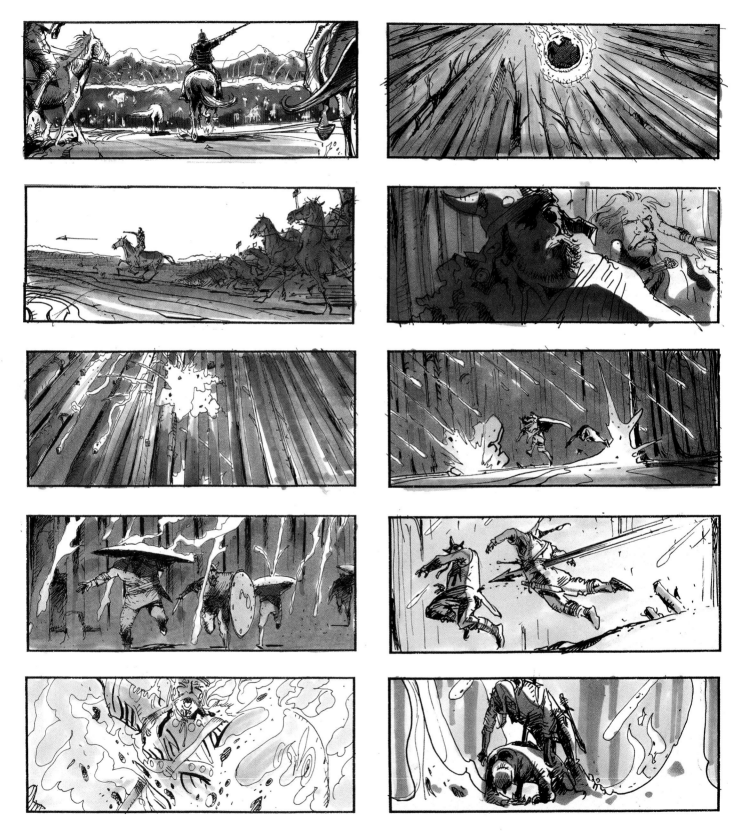

EXT. GERMAN FRONT - ROMAN OFFENSIVE LINE - DAY

> **MAXIMUS**
> Brothers, what we do in life. . . echoes in eternity ...

The soldiers operating the catapults pull back the arms so that the projectiles, pots of oil, can be loaded onto them.

> **CATAPULT SOLDIER**
> Catapults ready, sir!

A flaming arrow is launched by the Germans.

> **ARCHER COMMANDER**
> Archers, ignite!

An archer strings a cloth-tipped arrow, the foot soldier lights it, the archer draws his bow, and fires. All the cavalry look up. The flaming arrow sings into the air—up—up—

Quintus sees the flaming arrow rise over the tree-tops. Behind him stands the line of ARCHERS, the Scorpions, the battery of mighty catapults, loaded and strained back to maximum tension.

> **QUINTUS**
> Now!

The catapults are released, hoisting up into the air a hundred bulbous terra cotta pots that curve up, up, in a high arc towards the trees. Quintus counts off the seconds as they fly.

> **QUINTUS** (*cont'd*)
> One ... two ... three ... four ... Now!

The Scorpion teams release their shower of deadly bolts into the sky.

QUINTUS (*cont'd*)
One ... two ... Now!

The archers raise fire-tipped arrows and fire their flaming barrage into the sky.

Quintus raises his sword arm and signals the advance. The entire Roman line of foot soldiers begins to move steadily forward.

EXT. TREES - CAVALRY POSITION - DAY

Screaming out their blood-curdling war-cry, Maximus spurs his horse into the charge. The entire regiment of cavalry takes up the howling cry and charges alongside him— building up speed...

EXT. BATTLEFIELD - TREES - DAY

... straight at the wall of fire that was once the trees—hammering over the uneven ground ... At full gallop now—they SLAM into the flames—

MAXIMUS

Stay with me!

EXT. BATTLE FIELD - DAY

The Roman foot soldiers move relentlessly forward in their lines, slashing with their short swords, but the Germans are fighting for their lives, doing terrible damage—the fight is degenerating into a muddy mutual slaughter.

Out of the flames, at full gallop, bursts Maximus and his screaming cavalry. The Germans turn in terror, caught between two walls of death—and the horsemen are upon them, cutting them down.

INT. ROMAN CAMP - MARCUS'S CHAMBER - NIGHT

Commodus enters the Imperial tent. Moves toward a marble bust of Marcus, touches it.

MARCUS (O.S.)
Are you ready to do your duty for Rome?

Commodus turns to face his father.

COMMODUS
Yes, father.

MARCUS
You will not be Emperor.

Commodus freezes as he hears this. It's a thunderbolt, but he manages to control his expression, as his mind races.

COMMODUS
Which wiser, older man is to take my place?

MARCUS
My powers will pass to Maximus, to hold in trust until the Senate is ready to rule once more. Rome is to be a republic again.

COMMODUS
Maximus ...

Marcus reaches out to touch Commodus's face and Commodus pulls back.

MARCUS (cont'd)
My decision disappoints you.

Beat.

COMMODUS
You wrote to me once, listing the four chief virtues. Wisdom, justice, fortitude, and temperance. As I read the list, I knew I had none of them. But I have other virtues, Father. Ambition. That can be a virtue when it drives us to excel. Resourcefulness. Courage. Perhaps not on the battlefield, but there are many forms of courage. Devotion. To my family, to you. But none of my virtues were on your list. Even then, it was as if you didn't want me for your son.

MARCUS (Deeply saddened)
Oh, Commodus, you go too far.

COMMODUS (sobbing now)
I search the faces of the gods for ways to please you ... to make you proud ... I can never do it. One kind word, one full hug where you pressed me to your chest and held me tight would have been like the sun on my heart for a thousand years. What is it in me you hate so much?

MARCUS
Shh, Commodus.

COMMODUS
All I've ever wanted was to live up to you. Caesar. Father.

Commodus cannot control his tears. Marcus, much moved, kneels before his son and holds up his arms.

MARCUS
Commodus. Your faults as a son ... is my failure as a father.

Commodus enters his embrace, kissing the top of his father's head, weeping freely. Then he presses his father's head to his chest.

COMMODUS
I would butcher the whole world, if you would only love me ...

He holds his father's face tight against his chest, suffocating him.

Marcus begins to struggle, but Commodus holds his head in an iron grip, the tears still rolling down his cheeks. He doesn't relax his hold until he feels the old man's body drop limp in his arms.

AFRICA

Half dead from exhaustion when he reaches home, Maximus comes face to face with worst nightmare. His farm lies in smoking ruins, his wife and son are charred corpses nailed to crosses. The Praetorians got there first. Local brigands, drawn like vultures by the smoke, find the half-conscious Maximus and carry him off a prisoner, soon to be transported across the Mediterranean and sold into slavery in North Africa.

But no ordinary slave: Maximus soon finds himself in a provincial market town with a wagonload of other able-bodied male captives fated to become gladiators. Along with Juba, a Numidian plucked from the Carthage salt mines, and several others, he is purchased by the veteran gladiator trainer Proximo. During "boot camp" at Proximo's compound, Maximus refuses to fight and speaks to no one. Juba, intrigued by this proud, quiet man, tends his wounds and slowly draws him out. And when Maximus and Juba are thrown into vicious combat in the arena—each pair of gladiators chained together at the wrist—they fight as a team and survive by slaying all who attack them.

Proximo then realizes that "the Spaniard" is something he hasn't seen for a while: not just a natural fighter but a trained warrior, and a man with an indomitable spirit. But he remains puzzled by Maximus's indifference to his growing reputation in the provincial arena. Meanwhile, Proximo has learned that the new emperor, Commodus, has decreed an important round of gladiatorial games, ironically to commemorate his late father. And Maximus, if he will commit, can be Proximo's ticket out of the small time and back to Rome.

Revealing that he himself once fought as a gladiator and was awarded his freedom by the great Marcus Aurelius years earlier, Proximo hooks Maximus with the promise that, if he's good enough, he too will stand before the emperor one day. This is all Maximus needs to hear. He lives only to take revenge on Commodus, and if winning the crowd will put him within reach of his enemy, that's what he will do.

EXT. VINEYARD - MORNING

An unusual jingling sound is heard. Maximus appears to be dead.

The source of the jingling becomes clear when we see the feet of brigands, with delicate anklets, shuffling around him. A hand touches his sandals. Rich sandals. Another touches his tunic. Good cloth.

EXT. MONTAGE SEQUENCE - DAY/NIGHT

Fevered images come to Maximus as he sinks in and out of consciousness ... A harsh desert landscape passes ...

Maximus opens his eyes—a repulsive hyena is barking at him, jaws snapping—

The walls of his vineyards ... His hand skimming over the wheat stalks; a child's laughter in the distance ...

A large man, who we will know as Juba, is crouched close, smiling at Maximus ...

Maximus's hands skim over the dry stones of a desert ...

EXT. SLAVE WAGON TRAIN - DAY

Maximus's eyes slowly open.

Inches away from his face—straight down at him—the hyena snarls ...

His wife and son stand in a field ...

> **JUBA** (V.O.)
> Don't die ... You'll meet them again ...
> Not yet ...

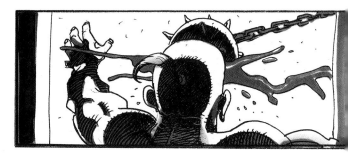
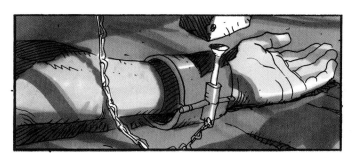
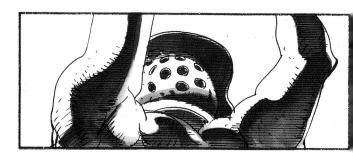

INT. TUNNEL, PROVINCIAL ARENA - DAY
Maximus "washes" his hands with a handful of earth, his pre-battle ritual.

The blacksmiths slam shackles on the gladiators' wrists, chaining them together in teams of two by a chain about four feet long. It's clear the method is to chain a "Red" to a "Yellow"—a good fighter to a certain loser.

EXT. ARENA - DAY
The crowd waits expectantly. The ANDABATAE warriors prepare to slaughter the gladiators.

INT. TUNNEL, PROVINCIAL ARENA - DAY
The gladiators wait at the gate to the arena. One of them is so frightened a puddle of urine is forming at his feet.

The doors to the arena swing open, silhouetting the waiting fighters in bright light. From the arena comes the sound of drums and the baying of a crowd eager for blood.

The line moves forward. Side by side, their chain dangling loose between them, Maximus and Juba stride into the arena.

EXT. PROVINCIAL ARENA - DAY
A dozen armored, very scary Andabatae thunder AT CAMERA. To the cheers of the crowd, they charge the chained teams, and the battle is on.

Haken fights with massive power, dragging his weeping partner after him. Juba fights well, fending off the howling attackers. Maximus surprises him by the effectiveness with which he blocks all attacks.

Haken's partner is killed. He hacks through the man's wrist and frees himself of the dead weight—now free to fight alone, he swings the chain as an additional weapon.

Maximus and Juba continue to make their stand, and every attacker that comes near them dies. It's an extraordinary display of teamwork, ice-cold nerve, and brute strength.

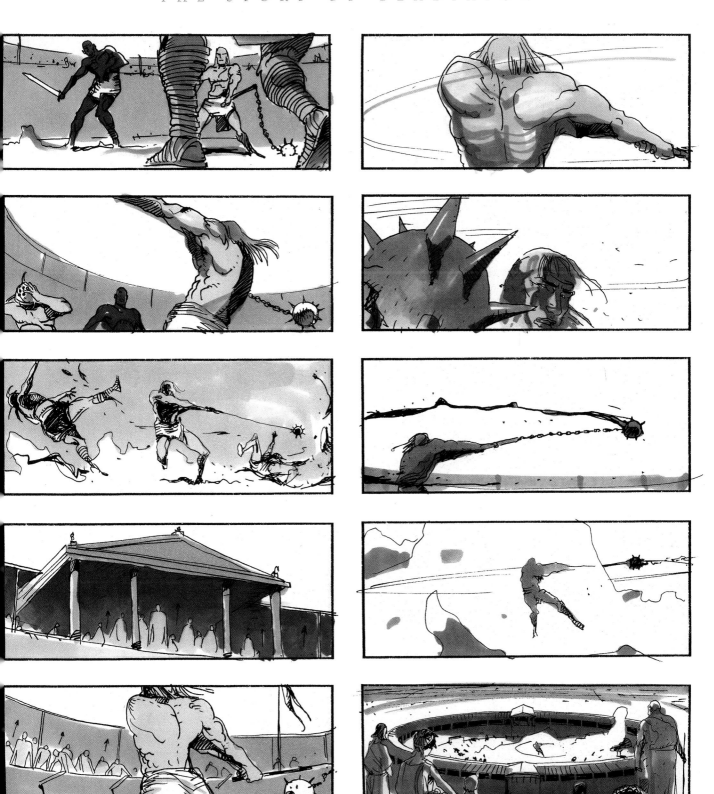

EXT. TERRACE, PROXIMO'S SCHOOL - EVENING
Proximo stands on a terrace overlooking his compound. Maximus stands before him.

PROXIMO
What do you want? Mm? Girl? Boy?

MAXIMUS
You sent for me.

Proximo sees the barely concealed lack of respect in the man who should be his slave.

PROXIMO
Yes, I did. You're good, Spaniard, but you're not that good. You could be magnificent.

MAXIMUS
I am required to kill. So I kill. That is enough.

PROXIMO
That's enough for the provinces, but not for Rome.

Proximo tosses a piece of food to a hyena chained in the corner.

PROXIMO (*cont'd*)
The young Emperor has arranged a series of spectacles to commemorate his father, Marcus Aurelius. I find that amusing, since it was Marcus Aurelius, the wise, the all-knowing

Marcus Aurelius that closed us down.

After a pause.

PROXIMO (*cont'd*)
Hmm ... So finally, after five years of scratching a living in flea-infested villages, we're finally going back where we belong. The Colosseum. Oh, you should see the Colosseum, Spaniard! Fifty thousand Romans watching every movement of your sword—willing you to make that killer blow— the silence before you strike—and the noise afterwards. It rises, rises up like, like a storm. As if you were the thunder god himself—

He stops, his eyes shining. Maximus sees it:

MAXIMUS
You were a gladiator.

Proximo turns unseeing eyes to him. Comes back to earth. Nods.

PROXIMO
Yes, I was.

MAXIMUS
You won your freedom?

PROXIMO
A long time ago, the Emperor presented me with a rudius—it's just a wooden sword—a symbol of your freedom. He touched me on the shoulder and I was free.

MAXIMUS (*laughing skeptically*)
You knew Marcus Aurelius?

PROXIMO
I did not say I knew him. I said he touched me on the shoulder once.

Beat.

MAXIMUS
You ask me what I want. I too want to stand before the Emperor, as you did.

PROXIMO
Then listen to me. Learn from me. I wasn't the best because I killed quickly.

I was the best because the crowd loved me!
Win the crowd, and you'll win your freedom.

Maximus thinks about this.

MAXIMUS
I will win the crowd. I will give them
something they've never seen before.

EXT. RAMPARTS, PROXIMO'S SCHOOL - EVENING

Maximus and Juba stand on the high ramparts,
looking out at the endless desert and the distant
mountains.

JUBA
It's somewhere out there—my country.
My home. My wife is preparing food ...
My daughters carry water from the river.
Will I ever see them again? I think, no.

MAXIMUS
Do you believe you'll meet them again—
when you die?

JUBA
I think so. But then—I will die soon. They
will not die for many years. I'll have to wait.

MAXIMUS
But you would ... wait.

JUBA
Of course.

Beat.

MAXIMUS
You see ... my wife ... and my son ... are
already waiting for me.

JUBA
You'll meet them again. But not yet, not
yet. Yes.

MAXIMUS
Yes ... not yet ...

ROME

As Proximo's gladiator transport rolls through the gates of Rome, the capital is uneasily getting used to its new emperor. Commodus shows open contempt for the Roman Senate and its leader, Gracchus. Lucilla, whom Commodus adores and depends on, adroitly tries to keep the peace but worries for the future of her young son, Lucius, next in line to the throne.

Maximus when the two were young, and had mourned him as lost.

As Maximus wins fight after fight, Commodus goes mad with frustration: he must destroy his foe but craves the approval of the Roman mob, who now worship Maximus. Heartened by the chance of a return to sane rule, Lucilla and Gracchus plot to free Maximus and reunite him

Proximo's gladiators, in their first appearance in the Colosseum, draw the role of doomed Carthaginians battling the Roman legions under Scipio Africanus. But Maximus, imposing military discipline on his men, wins a stunning victory. Commodus insists on meeting the mysterious "Spaniard"—and Maximus's true identity is revealed at last. The only person more shocked than Commodus is Lucilla, who was close to

with his troops to stage a coup. But Commodus uncovers and smashes the conspiracy, arrests Gracchus, and silences Lucilla by holding her son hostage. Vowing to rule Rome's heart, Commodus announces he will fight Maximus in single combat, but secretly and mortally wounds him before they engage. Even so, Maximus kills his tormentor with a supreme effort, and is released to join his loved ones in the afterlife.

INT. IMPERIAL PALACE - DAY

Gracchus is speaking to Commodus. The Senators are gathered there. Commodus toys with his sword restlessly as he listens. This has been going on for too long, and he's grown impatient. Lucilla sits to one side, listening, watching.

> **GRACCHUS**
> For your guidance, sire, the Senate has prepared a series of protocols to begin addressing the problems in the city—beginning with basic sanitation in the Greek Quarter, to combat the plague which is already springing up there. So if Caesar—

> **COMMODUS**
> Shh.

(he rises, paces)

> Don't you see, Gracchus, that's the very problem, isn't it? My father spent all his time at study. At books and learning and philosophy. He spent his twilight hours reading scrolls from the Senate. All the while, the people were forgotten.

> **GRACCHUS**
> The Senate is the people, sire. Chosen from among the people, to speak for the people.

> **COMMODUS**
> I doubt many of the people eat so well as you do, Gracchus. Or have such splendid mistresses, Gaius. I think I understand my own people.

> **GRACCHUS**
> Then perhaps Caesar will be so good as to teach us, out of his own extensive experience.

> **COMMODUS**
> I call it love. I am their father. The people are my children. And I shall hold them to my bosom, and embrace them tightly—

> **GRACCHUS**
> Have you ever embraced someone dying of plague, sire?

> **COMMODUS**
> No, but if you interrupt me again, I assure you that you shall.

Lucilla intervenes before it gets nasty.

> **LUCILLA**
> Senator, my brother is very tired. Leave your list with me. Caesar shall do all that Rome requires.

Commodus turns and strides off to the far side of the room. The Senators bow. Gracchus meets Lucilla's eyes with a smile. He respects her political skills

> **GRACCHUS**
> My lady. As always, your lightest touch commands obedience.

The Senators leave. Lucilla joins Commodus in the adjoining room

> **COMMODUS**
> Who are they to lecture me?

> **LUCILLA**
> Commodus. The Senate has its uses.

> **COMMODUS**
> What uses? All they do is talk. It should be just you, and me, and Rome.

LUCILLA
Don't even think it. There's always been a Senate.

COMMODUS
Rome has changed. It takes an Emperor to rule an empire.

LUCILLA
Of course. But leave the people their ...

She feels for the word.

COMMODUS
Illusions?

LUCILLA
Traditions.

But Commodus is running with a new thought.

COMMODUS
My father's war against the barbarians—he said it himself, it achieved nothing. But the people loved him.

LUCILLA
The people always love victories.

COMMODUS
Why? They don't see the battles. What do they care about Germania?

LUCILLA
They care about the greatness of Rome.

COMMODUS
The greatness of Rome! Well, what is that?

LUCILLA
It's an idea. Greatness ... greatness is a vision.

COMMODUS
Exactly! A vision! Do you not see, Lucilla? I will give the people a vision of Rome, and they'll love me for it. And they'll soon forget the tedious sermonizing of a few dry old men.

He reaches out his arm, takes her hand, and kisses it.

COMMODUS (*cont'd*)
I will give the people the greatest vision of their lives.

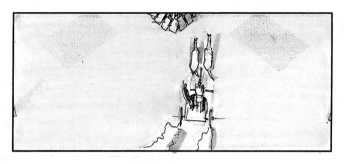

INT. ARENA

The crowd EXPLODES in cheers as the huge doors at one end of the arena suddenly burst open and six chariots thunder in. Each chariot has a driver and either an archer or a lanceman, both are dressed in theatrical versions of the familiar Roman Lorica Segmentata. There are also female warriors in bronze breastplates.

The chariots zoom around the outside of the arena, forcing the twenty gladiators toward the center. A cloud of dust obscures everything.

Maximus assesses the situation and their vulnerability. As the juggernauts spin around, he then turns around almost by instinct, and sees a spear flying through the dust—

The spear SLICES, into a gladiator's neck—killing him instantly—he falls, ungainly and hard. With no glory. . . .

Meanwhile, one chariot spins around and speeds straight into the gladiators' diamond—it SMASHES and tumbles—killing several gladiators in the mayhem.

The crowd is breathless—watching the final battle.

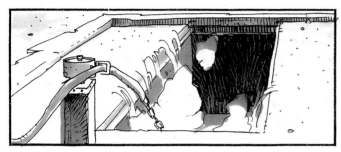

INT. COLOSSEUM, ARENA - DAY
The crowd cheers! Maximus appears from his gate. He carries a sword and a round shield.

Up in the Imperial Box, Commodus is watching Maximus closely.

> **COMMODUS**
> They embrace him like he's one of their own.

> **LUCILLA**
> The mob is fickle, brother—he will be forgotten in a month.

> **COMMODUS**
> No. Much sooner than that.

She looks, not quite understanding.

> **COMMODUS** (*cont'd*)
> It's been arranged.

Maximus looks at Tiger. Only one man with a sword and axe? Maximus picks up a handful of earth, rubs it between his hands.

> **TIGER**
> We who are about to die salute you!

Tiger lowers the visor on his elaborate silver

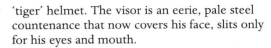'tiger' helmet. The visor is an eerie, pale steel countenance that now covers his face, slits only for his eyes and mouth.

Tiger kicks sand at Maximus and begins his attack. The sword play is very fast—they thrust and parry and hack like lightning, constantly attacking— they seem perfectly matched.

Then Maximus is knocked to the ground. Directly behind him, a vibration in the ground ... Suddenly trap doors swing open and a snarling Bengal tiger leaps to the arena floor, restrained by a chain. Tiger's teams of "cornermen" hold the chain through a pulley system. Maximus and Tiger continue to spar. Another trap door flies open—another tiger leaps to the floor.

And a third! And a fourth! The fierce tigers swirl about the two warriors as they fight, the corner-men tightening and loosening the slack of the chains. Maximus manages to knock Tiger's battle axe to the ground. The cornermen give one of the tigers more slack on its chain—it leaps on Maximus, who stabs the beast with his sword as it knocks him to the ground. The animal rolls off Maximus, dead. Tiger goes on the offensive again, and is about to get the upper hand when Maximus hacks him in the foot with the blade of his own

battle axe. Tiger screams in agony as blood spurts. Maximus kicks him to the sand. He uses the blade of the battle axe again, this time to lift the visor on Tiger's steel mask. The crowd is chanting "Kill! Kill!"—their thumbs pointing down, urging Maximus to chop off his head.

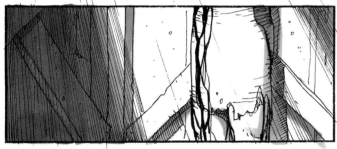

EXT. COLOSSEUM ARENA - DAY

Maximus falls to the sand. Lucilla is running across the arena to him. She drops to her knees.

> **LUCILLA**
> Maximus ...

Maximus's dying eyes flicker—he whispers to her—

> **MAXIMUS**
> Lucius is safe.

She is weeping, and whispers—

> **LUCILLA**
> Go to them.

Maximus' eyes close. His head tilts to the side. His body seems to drift, floating above the arena sands.

FLASH—MAXIMUS'S POV—The orchard—his wife and son stand waiting for him. His son spots him coming over a rise, runs toward him. Maximus strides through the wheat field toward his family...

He is gone. Lucilla lays his head down gently on the sand.

> **LUCILLA** (*cont'd*)
> You're home.

When she rises, the whole arena is watching her every move. She stands tall, and speaks to the Senators, only the occasional tremor betraying her emotion:

> **LUCILLA** (*cont'd, to* GRACCHUS)
> Is Rome worth one good man's life? We believed it once. Make us believe it again.

DreamWorks Pictures and
Universal Pictures present

A RIDLEY SCOTT Film
A DOUGLAS WICK Production

in association with

SCOTT FREE PRODUCTIONS

GLADIATOR

Directed by RIDLEY SCOTT

Screenplay by
DAVID FRANZONI and
JOHN LOGAN and
WILLIAM NICHOLSON

Story by DAVID FRANZONI

Produced by DOUGLAS WICK,
DAVID FRANZONI, BRANKO LUSTIG

Executive Producers
WALTER F. PARKES and
LAURIE MacDONALD

Director of Photography
JOHN MATHIESON

Production Designer ARTHUR MAX

Editor PIETRO SCALIA

Costume Designer JANTY YATES

Visual Effects Supervisor JOHN NELSON

Music by
HANS ZIMMER and LISA GERRARD

Casting by LOUIS DIGIAIMO

Associate Producer TERRY NEEDHAM

THE CAST

Maximus	RUSSELL CROWE
Commodus	JOAQUIN PHOENIX
Lucilla	CONNIE NIELSEN
Proximo	OLIVER REED
Marcus Aurelius	RICHARD HARRIS
Gracchus	DEREK JACOBI
Juba	DJIMON HOUNSOU
Falco	DAVID SCHOFIELD
Gaius	JOHN SHRAPNEL
Quintus	TOMAS ARANA
Hagen	RALF MOELLER
Lucius	SPENCER TREAT CLARK
Cassius	DAVID HEMMINGS
Cicero	TOMMY FLANAGAN
Tiger	SVEN-OLE THORSEN
Slave Trader	OMID DJALILI
Praetorian Officer	NICHOLAS McGAUGHEY

Scribe	CHRIS KELL
Assassin #1	TONY CURRAN
Assassin #2	MARK LEWIS
Valerius	JOHN QUINN
Praetorian Guard #1	ALUN RAGLAN
Engineer	DAVID BAILIE
German Leader	CHICK ALLEN
Giant Man	DAVE NICHOLLS
Rome Trainer #1	AL HUNTER ASHTON
Narrator	BILLY DOWD
Lucius' Attendant	RAY CALLEJA
Maximus' Wife	GIANNINA FACIO
Maximus' Son	GIORGIO CANTARINI
Stunt Coordinator	PHIL NEILSON
Maximus' Stunt Doubles	STUART CLARKE
	PETER WHITE
Maximus/Tiger Double	RANDY SCOTT MILLER

Stunts .... SEBASTIAN ABBATIELLO
EUGENIO ALONSO, CARLO ANTONIONI
BEN BELLMAN, GEORGES BRANCHE
MANUEL CABRERA, SERGIO CASADEI
ALESSANDRO CASALINO
VIKTOR CERVENKA, ALEJANDRO COBO
EUGENE COLLIER, GIANLUCA COPPETTA
FORBES COWAN, RICARDO CRUZ
MICHEL DIDIER, WALTER DIFRANCESCO
PETER DROZDA, ZDENEK DVORACEK
MOHAMMED ENAHAL, NEIL FINNIGHAN
KAMIL FOJTIK, ALEJANDRO GARCIA
JOSS GOWER, CARLTON HEADLEY
ANDY HRIC, MARTIN HUB
CHARLES JARMAN, CHUCK JEFFREYS
KEVIN JOHNSON, MORGAN JOHNSON
RADOWAN KAK, VINCENT KEANE
IVO KRISTOF, MICHAEL IAN LAMBERT
DEREK LEA, STEPHANE LELIEVRE
MIROSLAV LHOTKA, GUY LIST
TREVOR LOVELL, TONY LUCKEN
TOM LUCY, ROBBIE MacFARLANE
CHRIS MANGER, IVAN MICA
PETER MILES, GRAHAM MULLINS
MUSTAPHA NATOURI, MIROSLAV NAVRATIL
MARK NEWMAN, RAY L. NICHOLAS
PETER OLGYAY, JANE OMOROGBE
HERNAN ORTIZ, PAULINE RICHARDS
MARC ROBERTS, JEAN-PHILLIPE ROMAN
KEN SCOTLAND, JOSE MARIA SERRANO
DAVID SLAIVRE, C. C. SMIFF
GORDON SMITH, BRIAN SMYJ
EDDIE STACEY, R. J. STEEL
JENNIFER STOUTE, MAREK TOTH
MARTIN UHROVCIK, PAVEL VOKOUN
IAN WALKER, SEORAS WALLACE
DAVID WEISS, TUBARDH WILSON

THE CREW

Unit Production Manager	BRANKO LUSTIG
First Assistant Director	TERRY NEEDHAM
Second Assistant Director	ADAM SOMNER
Second Unit Director	
Second Unit Director	
of Photography	ALEXANDER WITT
Special Visual Effects by	MILL FILM, LONDON
Production Supervisor	TY WARREN
Unit Manager	JUDI BUNN

Set Decorator	CRISPIAN SALLIS
"A" Camera Operator	PETER TAYLOR
"B" Camera and	
Steadicam Operator	KLEMENS BECKER
"A" Camera Focus Puller	SIMON HUME
"B" Camera Focus Puller	SASCHA MIEKE
"A" Camera Clapper Loader	CRAIG BLOOR
"B" Camera Clapper Loader	TOM McFARLING
Clapper Loader	CIRO CANDIA
Camera Technician	AGAPIOS LOUKA
Still Photographer	JAAP BUITENDIJK
Script Supervisor	ANNIE WOTTON
Supervising Sound Editor	PER HALLBERG
Re-Recording Mixers	SCOTT MILLAN
	BOB BEEMER
Production Sound Mixer	KEN WESTON
Boom Operator	COLIN CODNER
Cableman	SAM STELLA
Video Operator	LESTER DUNTON
Chief Lighting Technician	ROGER LOWE
Assistant Chief Lighting Technician	ANDY COLE
Electricians	VIC CHANDLER
	GARY NAGLE
	FRED TODD
	DAVE McWHINNIE
Rigging Electrical Gaffers	LARRY PRINZ
	ALAN WILLIAMS
Rigging Electrical Best Boy	TERRY EDEN
Generator Operator	DAVID BRUCE
Key Grips	DAVID APPLEBY
	RUPERT LLOYD-PARRY
Best Boy Grip	ADRIAN McCARTHY
Camera Grip	PHIL MURPHY
Crane Operator	COLIN HAZELL
Property Master	GRAEME PURDY
Assistant Property Master	PETER HOOPER
Standby Props	MICKEY WOOLFSON
	KIERON McNAMARA
	STEPHEN McDONALD
	MICKEY PUGH (Consulting)
Dressing Props	
Supervisors	DENIS HOPPERTON
	MAURIZIO JACOPELLI (Italy)
	LUCIANO CECCOTI (Italy)
Dressing Props	WILLIAM HARGREAVES
	ROBERT SHERWOOD
	BEN WILKINSON
	STEVE PAYNE
	C. MacDONALD
	J. FOX
	PETER BIGGS
Senior Propmakers	ROLAND STEVENSON
	LEE BIGGS
	DAVID ATKINSON
	MALCOLM KEANE
Drapery Master	COLIN FOX
Drapesman	STEPHEN ASHBY
Buyer	LUCINDA STURGIS
Supervising Armourer	SIMON ATHERTON
Armourers	TOMMY DUNNE
	ALAN HAUSMANN
	WILLIAM ENGLEFIELD
	PAUL CASTLEMAN
Mr. Crowe's Armourer	IVO COVENEY
Special Effects & Prosthetic	
Supervisor	NEIL CORBOULD

Floor Supervisor .... PAUL CORBOULD
Special Effects .... JOHN EVANS
BARRY WHITROD
NORMAN BAILLIE
DAVE WATKINS
STEVE WARNER
LEE RIDER
SIMON QUINN
CAIMIN BOURNE
DAVE WILLIAMS
IAN CORBOULD
JASON McCAMERON
RAY LOVELL
TIM MITCHELL
ANNE MARIE WALTERS
Special Effects Assistant .... CAROL McAULAY
Animatronic Supervisor .... KEVIN HERD
Animatronic Designer ...... ASTRIG AKSERALIAN
Prosthetic Floor
    Supervisor .... MICHELLE TAYLOR
Prosthetic Designer .... JOHN SCHOONRAAD
Costume Supervisor ...... ROSEMARY BURROWS
Assistant Costume
    Designer .... SAMANTHA HOWARTH
Wardrobe Master .... WILLIAM McPHAIL
Mr. Crowe's Dresser .... MICHAEL CASTELLANO
Costumers .... TIM SHANAHAN
BRUNO DE SANTA
AMANDA TREWIN
WILLIAM STEGGLE
ANDREA CRIPPS
JOHN LAURIE
DAVE WHITEING
TIM GUTHRIE
PETER EDMONDS
NEIL MURPHY
ANABEL CAMPBELL
PETER HORNBUCKLE
RUPERT STEGGLE
DAVID EVANS
Key Makeup Artist .... PAUL ENGELEN
Makeup Artists .... TREFOR PROUD
MELISSA LACKERSTEEN
JO ALLEN
LAURA McINTOSH
Key Hair Stylist .... GRAHAM JOHNSTON
Hair Stylists .... CARMEL JACKSON
MARESE LANGAN
ANITA BURGER
ALEX KING
EMMA SHELDRICK
Production Coordinator ..... SALLIE BEECHINOR
Assistant Production
    Coordinator .... LESLEY KEANE
Production Controller .... JIM TURNER
Production Accountant .... CRYSTAL A. HAWKINS
Assistant Production Accountant ... HELENA RUIZ
Assistant Accountants .... BETTY WILLIAMS
SYLVIA MACKINTOSH
CARMEL CASSIDY
NOLAN MEDRANO
JOAN M. ZULFER
Post Production Accountant ..... MARIA DEVANE
Second Assistant Director .... HANNAH QUINN
Third Assistant Director .... EMMA HORTON
U.K. Casting by .... KATHLEEN MACKIE

U.S. Casting Associate ... STEPHANIE CORSALINI
Gladiator and Crowd Casting .... BILLY DOWD
Casting Assistant .... ROB MARTIN
Unit Publicist .... ROB HARRIS
Mr. Crowe's Dialogue Coach ... JUDI DICKERSON
Dialogue Coach .... SANDRA BUTTERWORTH
Fight Master .... NICHOLAS POWELL
Assistant Fight Master .... ANDREAS PETRIDES
Art Directors .... CLIFFORD ROBINSON (Vehicles)
FRANCO FUMIGALLI (Italy)
Assistant Art Director .... TIZIANO SANTI (Italy)
Location Manager........ SIMONA SERAFINI (Italy)
Production Illustrators .... SYLVAIN DESPRETZ
DENIS RICH
Construction Manager ...... MALCOLM ROBERTS
Pre-Viz Digital Designer................. JON BUNKER
Standby Painter .... PERRY BELL
Lettering and Decor Artists............... JIM STANES
CLIVE INGLETON
MONIKA GOLDSCHMIDT
Sculptors................................. JOHN ROBINSON
ROBERT WILLIAMS
RICHARD SMITH
JODY KING
EMMA JACKSON
Art Department
    Researcher .... BECKY LONGCRAINE
Standby Carpenter........................ MARK BRADY
Standby Rigger .... RICHARD LAW
Standby Stagehand .... EDDIE O'NEILL
Transportation Coordinator .... GERRY GORE
Chief Animal Trainer.... PAUL "SLED" REYNOLDS
Animal Trainer................ THIERRY LE PORTIER
Horse Master .... STEVE DENT
Assistant Horse Master .... PETER WHITE
Assistants to Mr. Scott .... JULIE PAYNE
MILLY LEIGH
ANNE LAI
Scott Free Executive ...... STEVEN KENT FOSTER
Consultant to Ridley Scott ... NEVILLE SHULMAN
Assistants to Mr. Parkes .... JOY JOHNSON
CORY C. MYLER
Assistant to Ms. MacDonald ...... LINDA KROLL
Assistants to Mr. Wick .... NANCY SAFRAN
DAVID A. SCHREIBER
Assistant to Mr. Lustig ... AMINTA TOWNSHEND
Assistant to Mr. Crowe .... ROBERT LONG
Assistant to Mr. Phoenix .... JEMMA KEARNEY
Mr. Crowe's Trainer .... RICK O'BRYAN
Set Production Assistant .... ANYA GRIPARI
PASCAL ROSSIGNOL
BENJAMIN HARRISON
MARK TAYLOR
Production Assistants .... DAVID OLIVER
CHRIS BURGESS
Projectionist .... LUCIEN NUNES-VAZ
Unit Nurse .... NICKY GREGORY
Post Production Executive .... MARTIN COHEN
Post Production
    Supervisor .... LISA DENNIS KENNEDY
Post Production
    Coordinator .... LISA MARIE SERRA
First Assistant Editors ...... CHISAKO YOKOYAMA
MICHAEL REYNOLDS
Assistant Editor .... FULVIO VALSANGIACOMO
Apprentice Editor .... STEVEN R. SACKS

Editorial Trainee .... BOB DRWILA
Visual Effects Editor .... WESLEY SEWELL
First Assistant Sound Editor ... KAREN M. BAKER
Supervising ADR Editor .... CHRIS JARGO
Supervising Foley Editor .... CRAIG JAEGER
Sound Effects Editors ... CHRISTOPHER ASSELLS
DINO R. DiMURO, M.P.S.E.
JON TITLE
RANDY KELLEY
Background Editor .... DAN HEGEMAN
Foley Editors .... RICHARD DWAN
LOU KLEINMAN
Dialogue Editors .... LAUREN STEPHENS
DAVID A. COHEN
SIMON COKE
ADR Editor .... LAURA GRAHAM
Assistant Sound Editors ...... PHILIP D. MORRILL
LEE W. LeBAIGUE
Assistant ADR Editor .... MICHELLE PAZER
Apprentice Sound Editor .... SHELLEY J. SMITH
Additional Audio .... MARK ORMANDY
MARK STOECKINGER
SCOTT GERSHIN
Foley Artists .... DAN O'CONNELL
JOHN CUCCI
JAMES MORIANA
JEFFREY WILHOIT
Foley Mixers .... JAMES ASHWILL
NERSES GEZALYAN
Foley Recordists .... LINDA LEW
GREG ZIMMERMAN
Foley Recorded at .... ONE STEP UP
VINE STREET STUDIOS
ADR Mixers .... THOMAS J. O'CONNELL
DEAN DRABIN
GREG STEELE
Additional Re-Recording
    Mixer .... FRANK MONTANO
Re-Recording Engineer ..... GARY L. G. SIMPSON
Machine Room for
    the Final Dub .... ANDREA LAKIN-ELISYAN
ROBIN JOHNSTON
Voice Casting .... L.A. MADDOGS
Sound Editorial Services
    provided by .... SOUNDELUX
Re-Recorded at .... TODD-AO WEST
Score Vocals formed by .... LISA GERRARD
COURTESY OF 4AD LTD.
Music Supervisor .... ADAM MILO SMALLEY
Executive in Charge of Music .... TODD HOMME
Music Editor .... DASHIELL RAE
Orchestrated by .... BRUCE L. FOWLER
YVONNE S. MORIARTY
and LADD McINTOSH
Score Co-Produced and
    Additional Music by .... KLAUS BADELT
Conducted by .... GAVIN GREENAWAY
London Music Coordinator MAGGIE RODFORD,
AIR EDEL & ASSOCIATES, LTD.
Music Recorded at .... AIR LYNDHURST
STUDIOS, LONDON
Music Recorded and Mixed by ... ALAN MEYERSON
Second Engineers .... NICK WOLLAGE
JAKE JACKSON
GREGG SILK
SLAMM ANDREWS

Second Engineers .... KEVIN GLOBERMAN
.... BRUNO ROUSSEL
Technical Score Advisors .... JUSTIN BURNETT
.... MARC STREITENFELD
Music Production Services ... MEDIA VENTURES
Orchestra Contracted by .... TONIA DAVALL
Copyist...................................... TONY STANTON
Assistants to
  Mr. Zimmer ..... MOANIKE'ALA NAKAMOTO
.... MICHAEL ALEXANDER
.... JIM DOOLEY
Title Design .... ROBERT DAWSON
Main Title .... DIGISCOPE
End Titles and Opticals .... PACIFIC TITLE
Negative Cutter .... KONA CUTTING
Color Timer .... DALE GRAHN
Technicolor London,
  Rushes Timer .... KEITH BRYANT

SECOND UNIT

Production Supervisors .... BRIAN COOK
.... ZDRAVKO MADZAREVIC
Second Assistant Director ... ADRIAN TOYNTON
"A" Camera Operator .... CLIVE JACKSON
"A" Camera Focus Puller ...... KEITH McNAMARA
"B" Camera Operator .... BRANKO KNEZ
"B" Camera Focus
  Puller .... ZORAN MIKINCIC BUDIN
Script Supervisor .... NADA PINTER
Video Operator .... JOHN BOWMAN
Grip .... MALCOLM HUSE

MALTA UNIT

Production Manager .... DRAGAN JOSIPOVIC
Unit Manager .... BRANKO JEHLAR
Supervising Art Director .... JOHN KING
Art Director .... PETER RUSSELL
Assistant Art Director .... ADAM O'NEILL
Set Decorator .... SONJA KLAUS
D & E Camera Operators .... BEN GOODER
.... FELIX SCHROER
Camera Focus Pullers .... NICK PENN
.... TIM FLEMMING
Clapper Loaders .... JAMES NEEDHAM
.... HOLGER JOOS
Electricians .... GIANCARLO McDONNELL
.... ZELJKO VRSCAK
.... DEAN BRKIC
.... VLADO CEH
.... ISTVAN DENC
.... DAMIR RADINOVIC
.... SAMIR KADRIC
.... STJEPAN VRBANIC
Generator Operator .... ALAN COATES
Grips .... DRAGO LJUBIC
.... VLADO RUKAVINA
.... JOSIP MATAUSIC
.... DUBRAVKO TOPOL
.... NENAD SOKAC
Property Master .... BRUCE BIGG
Props .... JAMES PARKER
.... PETR RICHTER
.... IVO UJEVIC
.... DOUG PURDY
Property Buyer .... LAWRENCE CAUCHI
Special Effects Supervisor .... TREVOR WOOD

Special Effects .... DAVE BRIGHTON
.... PETER WHITE
.... MIKE DURKAN
.... JOHN HERZBERGER
.... PETER FERN
.... STEVEN FOSTER
.... RAYMOND FERGUSON
.... CHRIS BENNAN
Special Effects Buyer .... CLIFF CORBOULD
Costumers .... MICHAEL MOONEY
.... YVONNE ZARB COUSIN
.... BRIDGET KENNINGHAM
.... MARIA HUBACKOVA
.... NADJA ALBERT
.... MARTA JENCOVA
.... HANA KUCEROVA
.... JANA JANKOVA
.... STANA SLOSSEROVA
Makeup Artists .... IVANA PRIMORAC
.... JULIA WILSON
.... ANA BULAJIK-CRECEK
Hair Stylists .... EVA WYEPLELOVA
.... IVANA NEMCVOVA
.... MARCELLE GENOVESE
Production Coordinator .... SANDRA ODELGA
Assistant Production
  Coordinator .... SNJEZANA TEPSIC
Maltese Consultant .... ALBERT GALEA
Maltese Coordinator .... MAVIS FORMOSA
Production Assistants .... ANDREW DEBONO
.... BRANO KOLLAR
.... DAVID BYRNE
Location Managers .... MIKE HIGGINS
.... PHILIP KOHLER
Construction Accountant MATTHEW O'TOOLE
Accountant .... CHRISTOPHER CONKLING
Assistant Accountant .... MICHAEL BEAUDIN
Payroll Accountant .... MARK BONICI
Accounting Assistant .... JENNIFER STIVALA
Draughtspersons .... HELEN XENOPOULOUS
.... TOAD TOZER
.... ANTHONY CARON-DELION
Art Department Production
  Assistants .... JODY KING
.... MICHELLE BORG
Assistant Construction
  Manager .... STEVEN FITZWATER
H.O.D. Painter .... BRIAN REILLY
H.O.D. Metal Worker ...... MICHAEL HOWLETT
H.O.D. Plasterer .... ROBERT VOYSEY
H.O.D. Carpenter ... GRAHAM BRUCE WEAMES
H.O.D. Rigger .... STEVE SANSOM
H.O.D. Stagehand .... KEITH SMITH
Transportation Manager ... DUBRAVKO PETROVIC
Assistant Transportation
  Manager .... ZDENKO SERTIC
Catering Supervisor .... ROBIN DEMETRIOU
Catering Provided by FIRST UNIT, CATERERS LTD.
Chariots & Horses
  Provided by ...... CAROZZE D'EPOCA, ROME
Tiger Trainers .... RANDY MILLER
.... CARMEL FLORES
Animal Handlers .... MONIQUE ANGEON
.... PIETRO ROSELLA
.... PASQUAL MARTINO
.... KAREN LE PORTIER

Production Services .... C&L LTD.
Velarium Shadow Design
  Engineers .... PETER HEPPEL and
.... PAUL ROMAINE of BURO HAPPOLD

U.K. UNIT

Supervising Art Director .... DAVID ALLDAY
Art Director .... KEITH PAIN
Set Decorator .... JILLE AZIS
Camera Focus Puller .... ASHLEY BOND
Camera Clapper Loader .... DEREK WALKER
Sound Cablemen .... RICHARD DANIELS
.... BENJAMIN BOBER
Generator Operator .... MARK HUTTON
Electrical Rigger .... NOBBY CLARKE
Props .... ANTHONY RYCYK
.... PAUL TURLEY
.... JOHN RUSSO
Assistant Construction Manager .... IAN GREEN
H.O.D. Props Painter .... MALCOLM KEANE
Supervising Armourer .... JOHN NIXON
Special Effects Supervisor .... DAVID HUNTER
Special Effects .... MIKE DUNLEAVY
.... STUART DIGBY
.... KENNETH HERD
.... IAN THOMPSON
.... PAUL DUNN
.... TIM STRACEY
.... DAVE MILLER
.... GRAHAM POVEY
.... COLIN UMPLEBY
.... ALAN YOUNG
.... PAUL TAYLOR
.... JOHN PILGRIM
Costumers .... BRIAN LAWLER
.... MIKE SKORZEPPA
.... STEVE KIRBY
Accounting Assistants .... TABITHA BURRILL
.... JEAN SIMMONS
.... JULIAN MURRAY
Location Manager .... TERRY BLYTHER
Assistant Location Managers ..... MARK SOMNER
.... NICHOLAS WALDRON
Second Second
  Assistant Director .... ROBERT WRIGHT
Third Assistant Director .... GARY TALBOT
Scenic Artists .... ROBERT WALKER
.... CYNTHIA SADLER
.... BRIAN BISHOP
.... DOUGLAS BISHOP
Draughtspersons .... NICK PALMER
.... JULIE PHILPOTT (Set Dressing)
.... SHARON CARTWRIGHT (Set Dressing)
Set Decorating
  Assistants .... KATY HENDERSON
.... NICOLA DE FRESNES
Set Dressing Buyer .... GINA CROMWELL
Art Department Production
  Assistants .... CLAIRE RICHARDS
.... HARRY PAIN
Drapery .... EDDIE REES
.... CHRIS WEST
.... COLIN PEARCE
Greensman .... ROGER HOLDEN
Catering Manager .... DAVID REYNOLDS
Catering Provided by .... SET MEALS LTD.

Rome Technical Advisor .... JOHN EAGLE
Stand-Ins .... AIDAN HARRINGTON
    COLLETTE APPLEBY
    PATRICK FLANAGAN
    MARK FISHER
    JIM DURBAN
    NICKY WHITE
Assistant Editors .... CHRIS WOMACK
    PAUL ELMAN
AVID Assistant .... VALERIO BONELLI
Apprentice Editor .... ANDREW HAIGH
Editorial Trainee .... KAREN HURLEY

MOROCCO UNIT
Production Managers .... PETER HESLOP
    ZAK ALAOUI
First Assistant Director .... AHMED HATIMI
Supervising Art
    Director .... BENJAMIN FERNANDEZ
Assistant Art Directors .... JOSE LUIS DEL BARCO
    CARLOS BODELON
Set Decorator .... ELLI GRIFF
Assistant Set
    Decorator .... JEAN-CHARLES VENET
"A" Camera Focus Puller .... EAMONN O'KEEFFE
Camera Assistants .... BRAHIM AIT BELKAS
    DRISS AYAD
Video Assist .... EL MOKHTAR ABOUKAL
Electricians .... ABDELLATIF EL ANSARY
    ISMAIL EL MOULLOUA
    ABDELKADER BENOUNA
    HICHAM BOUCHTA
    TAHAR AJOUALIL
    MOHAMMED RAMI
Grips .... ABDENAZIZ BIZZI
    MUSTAPHA EL IDRISSI
Crane Operator .... PAUL LEGALL
Property Master .... PHILIP McDONALD
Props .... LAHOUCINE JAOUD
    MOHAMMED ZRAR
Property Buyer .... ABDELKRIM RAISS
Drapery .... CAROLINE SINA
    ABDERARRAHIM EL HAJLI
Special Effects Supervisor .... TERRY GLASS
Special Effects .... MARK MEDDINGS
    JEFF CLIFFORD
    PETER SKEHAN
    ABDELLAH JOUDI
    HANIN OUIDDER
    MOHAMMED AQERMIM
    EL HASSAN TIB
Wardrobe Supervisors .... SARAH TOUAIBI
    ABDELKRIM AKKELLACH
Costumers .... SAID GHAINE
    HASSAN TAGHRITI
    MOHAMMED FALAHI
    MOHAMMED HARSHI
    ABDELFATAH QZAIBAR
    AIT HAMID ABDELLAM
    MOHAMMED RAJ
Makeup Assistants .... KHALID ALAMI
    LATIFA SOUIHI MAADANI
    HAYAT OULED DAHHOU
Hair Stylist .... SAID AHMED EL GROUNE
Hair Assistants .... BRAHIM NAAIM
    AICHA EL MEZIANE

Production Coordinators .... WINNIE WISHART
    KHADIJA KOULLA
Production Secretary .... JINANE BEN ZAIDA
Accountant .... KEVIN GREENE
Assistant Accountant .... MYRIAM TAYEBI
Accounting Assistant ABDESSALAM AIT ABDELAH
Location Managers .... JEREMY JOHNS
    ALI BAKKIOUI EL OTMANI
    MOHAMMED BENHMAMANE
Second Assistant
    Directors .... ZINEDINE IBNOU JABAL
    ALI CHERKAOUI
    MOHAMED NASRATE
Casting
    Draughtsperson ....ALEJANDRO FERNANDEZ
    BERNALDO DE QUIROS
Art Department Production
    Assistant .... SAMIRI MENOUER
Transportation Manager .... HAMID ARAISSI
Assistant Transportation
    Manager .... NAJMA EL MAHJOUB
Animal Trainers .... FESS REYNOLDS
    DEANN ZARKOWSKI
    KATHY PIRELLI
Production Assistants .... TARIQ AIT BEN ALI
    INSA FE
    KHALID BANOUJAAFAR
    MUSTAPHA ADIDOU
    ABDERHMANE
    ID-IDDER
Production Services, Morocco .... DAWLIZ S.A.

MILL FILM, LTD.
Visual Effects Supervisors .... TIM BURKE
    ROB HARVEY
Visual Effects Producer .... NIKKI PENNY
Executive Producer .... ROBIN SHENFIELD
Production Executive .... NANCY ST. JOHN
CG Supervisor .... LAURENT HUGUENIOT
Visual Effects Coordinators ...... EMMA NORTON
    LOREA HOYE
Production Coordinator, U.S.A. ... DIANA STULIC
Mill Film FX Editor .... SCOTT ANDERSON
Chief of Technology .... BILL SCHULTZ
Compositors .... HANI ALYOUSIF
    IAN PLUMB
    SIMON STANLEY-CLAMP
    KLAUDIJA CERMAK
    MIKE CONNOLLY
    JOHN HARDWICK
    MICHAEL ILLINGWORTH
    RICHARD ROBERTS
    LOUISE LATTIMORE
    STEVE MURGATROYD
Digital Matte Painters .... DAVE EARLY
    MICHELE MOEN
    SIMON WICKER
Digital Preparation .... HUONG DAM
    SANDRA ROACH
Lead CG Artists .... ROB ALLMAN
    ANDY KIND
    IVOR MIDDLETON
    BEN MORRIS
    TIM ZACCHEO
CG Artists .... PHIL BORG
    NICOLA BRODIE

CG Artists .... KEVIN MODESTE
    CRAIG PENN
    CHRIS SHAW
    GABRIEL WHITE
Additional CG .... GRAHAME ANDREW
    ALISON LEAF
Software Development Lead .... DAVE LOMAX
Additional Software
    Development .... KEVIN CAMPBELL
    JOHN STRAUSS
Systems Support .... JOHNATHAN BRAZIER
    JOHN FRITH
    DR. DAVID GREGORY
I/O Supervisor .... TIM CAPLAN
Colour Timer .... COLIN COULL
TA Managers .... MARILYN ANDERSON
    STEPHEN ELSON
Filmout Operators .... STEVE BARNES
    LEIGH RABY
Technical Assistants .... ALI BERNARD
    WILL BROADBENT
    JOYCE LAURENT
    STEVE PARSONS
    CHARLEY HENLEY
Editorial Assistant .... NICHOLAS ATKINSON
Additional VFX Editing .... JIMMY WEEDON
Visual Effects Camera Operator ... STEVEN HALL
Visual Effects Camera
    Assistant .... DAVID MATCHES
Grip Operator .... JIM CROWTHER
Digital Mix & Overlay .... CASPAR GORDON
Studio Effects Shoot
    Cameraman .... MALCOLM WOOLDRIDGE
Studio Effects Shoot Assistant ...DIGNA NIGOUMI
Gaffer .... STEVE DAVIS
Rigger .... PAT KILLEEN
Motion Capture Studio .... AUDIOMOTION
Visual Effects Assistant
    Coordinator .... PAUL EDWARDS
Production Assistant .... DOM SIDOLI
Production Runner .... AARON PAUL
Production Accountant .... NEIL HUGHES
Accounts Assistant,
    Mill Film, L.A. .... LAYA ARMIAN

The producers wish to thank the following for
their assistance in making this film:

South East England Forest District
The People of Farnham, Surrey, United Kingdom
The Government and People of Morocco
The Government and People of Malta
Mestiere Cinema, Venice
Professor Kathleen Coleman of Harvard University

Filmed in the United Kingdom,
Morocco, Malta and Italy

"Pavor" & "Etruria" Written by Walter Maioli &
Natalia Van Ravenstein. Performed by Synaulia.
Courtesy of Amiata Media Srl.

ACKNOWLEDGMENTS

Permission to reprint copyrighted material from the following sources is gratefully acknowledged. The publisher has made every effort to contact copyright holders; any errors or omissions are inadvertent and will be corrected upon notice in future reprintings.

Portions of the text of this book are excerpted or adapted from original articles by Joe Fordham that appeared in *VFXPro,* an online publication of Creative Planet, Inc. For the complete articles, go to www.VFXPro.com, keyword Gladiator.

PAGE 18: Production still photo from *Spartacus,* produced by Universal Studios. PAGE 19: Poster art for *Ben-Hur,* produced by Metro Goldwyn-Mayer (MGM) Studios. Courtesy of Warner Bros. Promotional still photo for *Quo Vadis?,* produced by Metro Goldwyn-Mayer (MGM) Studios. Courtesy of Warner Bros. PAGE 20: Promotional still photo for *The Last Days of Pompeii.* Courtesy Columbia Pictures Television. Production still photo from *Ben-Hur,* produced by Metro Goldwyn-Mayer (MGM) Studios. Courtesy of Warner Bros. PAGE 21: Promotional still photo for *Cleopatra,* produced by 20th Century Fox. PAGES 24–25: Jean-Léon Gérôme, *Pollice Verso ("Thumbs Down").* Phoenix Art Museum, Museum Purchase. PAGE 42: Portrait bust of the Emperor Commodus. Photo Scala / Art Resource, NY. PAGE 64: Lawrence Alma-Tadema, *Spring.* The J. Paul Getty Museum, Los Angeles. PAGE 90: Jean-Léon Gérôme, *The Death of Caesar.* The Walters Art Gallery, Baltimore.

The publisher thanks the following for their special contributions to this book:

Corinne Antoniades, Melissa Baldwin, Susan Bennett, Sharon Black, Alison Clarke, Kristy Cox, Paul Elliott, Anne Globe, Paul Lister, Laurie MacDonald, Vivan Mayer, Andrea McCall, Cory Mylar, Boyd Peterson, Jennifer Porter, Jennifer Rubin, and Dorit Saines at DreamWorks.

Production designer Arthur Max, visual effects supervisor John Nelson, and production illustrator Sylvain Despretz for their invaluable contributions of time and information about the *Gladiator* production.

Beth Vitallo of Scott Free Productions.

Joe Fordham, Suzanne Lezotte, Amy Barraclough, and Morgan Newman of Creative Planet, Inc.

Keith Hollaman, Frank DeMaio, Ann Lee, and Kelli Taylor at Newmarket Press; Timothy Shaner of Night & Day Design; and Diana Landau of Parlandau Communications—Words by Design.

Our deepest thanks to director Ridley Scott, executive producer Walter Parkes, and screenwriter David Franzoni for their generous contributions to this book.